teach® yourself

owning a cat

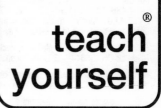

owning a cat
andrea mchugh

For over 60 years, more than 50 million people have learnt over 750 subjects the **teach yourself** way, with impressive results.

be where you want to be
with **teach yourself**

For UK order enquiries: please contact Bookpoint Ltd, 130 Milton Park, Abingdon, Oxon, OX14 4SB. Telephone: +44 (0) 1235 827720. Fax: +44 (0) 1235 400454. Lines are open 09.00–17.00, Monday to Saturday, with a 24-hour message answering service. Details about our titles and how to order are available at www.teachyourself.co.uk

For USA order enquiries: please contact McGraw-Hill Customer Services, PO Box 545, Blacklick, OH 43004-0545, USA. Telephone: 1-800-722-4726. Fax: 1-614-755-5645.

For Canada order enquiries: please contact McGraw-Hill Ryerson Ltd, 300 Water St, Whitby, Ontario, L1N 9B6, Canada. Telephone: 905 430 5000. Fax: 905 430 5020.

Long renowned as the authoritative source for self-guided learning – with more than 50 million copies sold worldwide – the **teach yourself** series includes over 500 titles in the fields of languages, crafts, hobbies, business, computing and education.

British Library Cataloguing in Publication Data: a catalogue record for this title is available from the British Library.

Library of Congress Catalog Card Number: on file.

First published in UK 2006 by Hodder Education, 338 Euston Road, London, NW1 3BH.

First published in US 2006 by The McGraw-Hill Companies, Inc.

This edition published 2006.

The **teach yourself** name is a registered trade mark of Hodder Headline.

Copyright © 2006 Andrea McHugh

Illustrations by Glennis Johns

Typeset by Transet Limited, Coventry, England.
Printed in Great Britain for Hodder Education, a division of Hodder Headline, 338 Euston Road, London, NW1 3BH, by Cox & Wyman Ltd, Reading, Berkshire.

The publisher has used its best endeavours to ensure that the URLs for external websites referred to in this book are correct and active at the time of going to press. However, the publisher and the author have no responsibility for the websites and can make no guarantee that a site will remain live or that the content will remain relevant, decent or appropriate.

Hodder Headline's policy is to use papers that are natural, renewable and recyclable products and made from wood grown in sustainable forests. The logging and manufacturing processes are expected to conform to the environmental regulations of the country of origin.

Impression number   10 9 8 7 6 5 4 3 2 1
Year   2010 2009 2008 2007 2006

contents

For my daughter, Madeline Joy, whose unconditional love sustains me always. Thanks also to her dad, William Mark Lainchbury, BVSc, MRCVS for his technical support and encouragement. And for Rufus, the most laid back cat I have ever known, who sadly died in 2005.

acknowledgements

Teach yourself about owning a cat

If you are considering whether or not to buy a cat or kitten but are wondering exactly what is involved and how this will affect your life, then this is the book for you.

While every cat is different, one thing is certain – as soon as you offer a cat a home your life will never be the same again. It is no coincidence that cats are associated with magic as they are certainly able to weave spells on people. As you begin to fall for their feline charms your needs will quickly become secondary to those of your cat, and you will enjoy catering for all his little quirks and fancies. Thankfully, a relationship with a cat is never a one-sided affair and in return you will find yourself rewarded with so much love, companionship and fun that your devotion will be a small price to pay.

Living with a cat provides a wonderful opportunity to observe and learn some valuable lessons about life. For a start there is the importance of regular relaxation and exercise. Cats know all about that. And there is much he can teach you about the art of looking gorgeous at all times while retaining just a hint of mystery and independence. You will soon realize that cats have very high standards when it comes to their owners. Fail to live up to these in any way and you will quickly encounter a disdainful glance and just a faint threat of, 'Sharpen your ideas up and look after me better, or I might just go and find someone who will!' With uncompromising attitudes like these, there is a lot we humans can learn from a cat.

One of the best things about living with a cat is that, no matter how stressful your day has been, coming home to his welcoming purr will have an instantly calming effect. All you have to do is shut the door, curl up together on the sofa and within minutes all that external stress will vanish and you will feel so much better. At least you will until he starts demanding his tea or bringing his toys for you to throw for him. One thing you will definitely learn is that it is inadvisable and virtually impossible to ignore a cat. But more of that later ...

There is a great deal to discover about the different life stages of a cat as he passes from that 'oh so cute' kitten stage into a beautiful adult cat and eventually into a (hopefully) serene old age puss (OAP). Kittens, with their love of life, instinctive curiosity and sense of fun will hook people into their lives from the very beginning. However, as beautiful as all kittens are they are also incredibly vulnerable and depend on their owners completely to nurture and help them develop into the sleek, confident adult cats they deserve to be.

Owning a cat is a wonderful adventure but it is also a big undertaking and responsibility, so here is a word of warning. Some breeds of cat never lose their kitten-like joie-de-vivre and see it as their duty to entertain you and act the clown throughout their lives. While that can sound amusing, in reality it can also be somewhat exhausting. Before taking on a livewire kitten like this it is important to take stock of the time and resources you have available and to be honest about your own personality type. No matter how much you fall in love with the look of a kitten, you may not have the emotional or physical resources to take on or cope with a high maintenance cat for the next 18+ years. Sadly, rescue centres are full of cats in need of rehoming because their owners did not take a few hours to research the type of cat that would best suit their lifestyle. This is a heartbreaking situation that can easily be avoided by following my step-by-step guide to choosing a kitten.

Throughout each stage of your cat's life his needs will be constantly changing. For example, an OAP will bring a new perspective and enjoyment to your life but like all the other life stages, this is a period that will not be without its challenges. Just like an ageing relative who has lived with you for many years, your OAP may suddenly become calmer and more peaceful or he may surprise you by becoming downright grumpy and demanding!

Coping with these behaviour and personality changes can be difficult. Increased health problems and visits to the vet can also be worrying. The good news is that with a little forward planning and extra care you can help enrich and enhance your cat's life so that he remains happy and comfortable and you can both enjoy these later years to the maximum. Achieving this can bring an owner real pleasure and a deep sense of satisfaction. The knowledge that you have done everything you possibly can for your cat throughout each stage of his life will also bring you comfort when the time eventually comes for you to say goodbye to each other.

Teach Yourself Owning a Cat will take you by the hand and help you to understand the physiological and emotional changes that are happening throughout your cat's life. Taking time to do this will ensure that owners and cats can enjoy living purrfectly happily in peace and harmony. This is the book that your cat will most want you to read, so let's get started!

01

owning a kitten

In this chapter you will learn:
- owner responsibilities
- about pedigrees and moggies
- how to choose a kitten.

Family planning

Cats are truly beautiful creatures and make such wonderful, loving companions that it is no surprise they are more popular than ever as household pets. However, it would be unrealistic to assume that everyone is enamoured by cats. Getting a kitten should be always be a joint family decision, as he will hopefully go on to become an important member of your family for the next 15–20 years.

Before you commit to taking on a kitten there are many things that you need to consider including the reason you really want a kitten, and whether or not you have the appropriate time, money and facilities that he is going to need.

Let's begin with that first, important question. Why do you want a kitten? Have you thought whether you would be better equipped to offer a home to an older cat? Some of the reasons that people are so determined they would like a kitten in their lives include:

- For companionship
- To have something small and cute to love
- To be a part of every stage of its life
- As a baby substitute
- To replace a lost pet
- To fulfill a childhood dream.

With their big blue eyes and playful ways all kittens are adorable, but this cute stage of kittenhood passes all too quickly and they soon grow into adult cats that look and behave quite differently. This is why it is very important to do your research so that you select exactly the right cat for you and ensure he is one that you will be able to bond with and care for through all the stages of his life.

If anyone in your family is uncertain about whether they are prepared to share their home with a kitten, it is better to be honest about this from the start and, if necessary, delay the decision until the time is right. Disappointed as you may be, do not be tempted to buy a kitten as a surprise, or dismiss someone else's opinion and go ahead and get one anyway. Rescue shelters are full of cats and kittens who were bought and returned as unwanted gifts.

It may be possible for you to help a family member to overcome their worries, perhaps by chatting any concerns through or taking them to a cat show to observe examples of a breed you are interested in but if someone suffers from severe allergies or is worried that in reality no one will have enough time and resources to care for the cat, then it is much better to acknowledge this and wait until your situation has changed.

Did you know?

The word 'kitten' was first recorded in the English language in 1377 and is thought to originate from the Turkish word for cat, which is *keti* or *kedi*.

Responsibilities of an owner

Cats have the reputation of being extremely independent creatures but in fact this is a complete myth. Domestic cats rely on their owners for almost every aspect of their care. You need to be sure you can be provide the cat with:

- A nutritionally balanced diet
- Fresh water every day
- A litter tray and cat litter
- Quality time, to care for the cat and interact with him
- Grooming – some cats are considered much higher maintenance than others
- Veterinary and dental care – at least an annual check-up, plus worming and flea treatments
- Vaccinations
- Microchipping
- Somewhere warm and draught-free to sleep
- Scratch posts
- An area that he can safely retreat to if he feels insecure or threatened
- Exercise facilities such as a safe garden or outdoor run
- Provision for his care when you are away on holiday or unexpectedly home late from work.

Did you know?

We are now living in such a cat crazy world that there are an estimated 500 million pet cats across the entire globe! In the USA around 60 million cats are kept as pets with 37 per cent of households owning at least one. In the UK there are about 7 million pet cats and they are now more popular than dogs, with one in four households owning at least one pet puss. In Australia, about 26 per cent of houses have at least one cat and in Canada, there are about 5 million domestic cats.

Kittens and kiddies

Take into consideration any children you have, or are planning to have, *before* you get a kitten. It is very important that a kitten should not become a baby substitute, as too much pampering can lead to health, emotional and behavioural problems that can impact on everyone in the house.

Research has repeatedly shown that pet ownership is good for children in almost every way. It makes them less self-centred, and teaches them about taking responsibility for a living creature and also the realities of coping with grief and loss should anything happen to the pet. Some studies in the USA have shown that owning a pet such as a cat can help children recover more quickly from physical or emotional trauma such as divorce or physical abuse.

Toxoplasmosis

On the down side, it is a fact that cats can infect pregnant women with toxoplasmosis, which can affect the unborn foetus. Toxoplasma is a single-celled parasite found in almost all mammals but cats are significant in its life cycle. Other sources of toxoplasmosis infection to humans include handling soiled vegetables or meat.

It is not necessary to get rid of a kitten or cat when you become pregnant, and it is certainly something that should have been discussed during the initial decision-making process. Pregnant women can still safely keep cats provided they undertake a strict hygiene regime, particularly when handling litter trays or gardening. You can get expert advice from your doctor or midwife, and a blood test at the start of the pregnancy and towards the end will help to put your mind at rest. It is important to remember that stroking and playing with a healthy cat will not make you ill and can be just as calming during pregnancy as at any other time.

To prevent infection with toxoplasmosis you should:

- Always wear gloves when cleaning out litter trays or working in the garden.
- Clean litter trays daily, disposing of faeces in a tied plastic bag in an outdoor dustbin. There are some compostable cat litters available, but check the labelling on packaging carefully. Never put cat faeces directly onto a compost heap.
- Wash hands thoroughly before handling any food.
- Feed the cat cooked meat only.
- Wash all fruit and vegetables before eating.
- Discourage your cat from catching vermin such as mice.
- Teach children to wash their hands after handling the cat.

Top Cat Tip

Cats can view children's sandpits as giant litter trays that have been placed in the garden for their personal convenience! Make sure that sandpits have a lid and are covered up when not in use, to prevent any cats from investigating and going in there.

Child care

Encourage your children to become involved in caring for the kitten from the early stages. Even very young children can fetch his bowl from the cupboard or carry a box of cat biscuits over to you. Older children can take on responsibility for tasks such as washing and filling water bowls and learning to groom the cat. You must also teach them that although little kittens love to play, they need plenty of sleep as well and must be left alone for a nap and some 'down time' at regular intervals.

Show older children how to pick up and handle the kitten, teaching them to support him underneath but not squeeze him too tightly. Never leave your children alone with the kitten until you are confident that he is happy with them and nobody is likely to get hurt. If you have a baby in the house, always cover the cot or pram with a taut net that is strong enough to support the weight of a cat should he decide to jump in for a snooze. A cat will never intentionally hurt a baby but accidents can happen so avoid leaving them alone together.

Top Cat Tip

Keep your cat's food bowls off the floor after meal times, to avoid crawling babies sampling the delights of cat food! In addition, keep any veterinary medicines and products such as flea sprays locked safely away.

Did you know?

It is not just children who benefit from owning a cat or kitten. One study of owners over 55 reported that half of them said their cat made them act and feel younger and sprightlier, while more than half attributed greater happiness and health to the presence of a cat in the home. People over the age of 70 said that owning a cat forced them to get out more, if only to buy cat food, search for the cat or visit the vet.

Kittens and the working owner

Just because you work does not mean you cannot have a cat or a kitten but you will need to ensure that he is adequately cared for, exercised and entertained during the day. Avoid getting a kitten at a time when you have a lot of extra work on with tight deadlines or increased stress levels. This is a time that you want to be able to savour and enjoy, so wait until things have calmed down. You will then be able to provide the kitten with lots of attention and a regular routine for feeding, playing and grooming, etc. Here are some tips that can be used to help a busy, working owner:

- Before leaving for work, put down some dried food and fresh water so that your cat can eat and drink throughout the day. Ensure that a door is unable to slam shut denying him access to these.
- Provide him with some interactive toys that dispense treats as they are played with and rolled around. Hide a few treats around the house to encourage him to hunt for his food.

- If you are unable to return home during the day your kitten may become bored and under stimulated. If this is the case it may be better to consider getting two kittens, so that they can provide company and entertainment for each other. If possible, ask a cat-loving neighbour or friend to visit during the day, to feed or check on the cats. Alternatively, you can pay a professional animal sitter to provide this service.
- If your cat is to live permanently indoors you will have to provide him with plenty of toys and climbing frames or he could become bored and frustrated, which can lead to behaviour problems.
- Consider putting a cat flap into your door so that the cat has access to an outdoor run or a secure, safe garden area.
- When you return home at the end of the day, do not run in, then get changed for the gym and dash straight out. Make sure you give the kitten lots of fuss and attention, and then feed him before you do anything else.

Location, location

Have a good honest look at where you live and then try to imagine it from a cat or kitten's point of view. Some of the most important aspects of your new cat's home will include:

- How close are you to a busy road? If the answer is very close, it would not be fair to allow the kitten to go out unsupervised and risk being injured or killed by traffic. If this is the case you will need to opt for a cat that is happy to live indoors and consider providing him with an outdoor run, or train him to walk on a harness.
- Do you live in a rented apartment? Check with the landlord that you are allowed to keep a cat. Some will agree to this but could ask you to pay a small deposit to cover any extra cleaning or repair work that may need to be carried out at the end of your tenancy.
- What breeds are you considering? Some breeds are much more placid than others and happy to live indoors. Others (such as the hairless Sphynx) have special needs and would suffer from exposure to the elements if left outside.
- Do you live in the country? Are there lots of trees and fields for a cat to explore? If so, you may be able to offer a fun home to one of the more active breeds that enjoy climbing and playing outdoors.

• How many other cats are in the neighbourhood already? If there aren't any, try to find out your neighbours' views on cats before you get one. Some people really dislike cats and become very stressed if one strays into their garden. If so, you may be better getting an indoor cat rather than risk the wrath of an angry neighbour!

Indoor cats

Be aware that many breeders are so protective of their kittens that for various reasons they will refuse to sell them to anyone who intends to let them go outdoors! There are lots of breeds that are quite happy to live the indoor life. Most of the longhair breeds make ideal house cats, as do Ragdolls (semi-longhair) (see Plate 1) and Cornish and Devon Rexes (shorthair/curly coated). The Rexes are more active than Persians (see Plate 2) and Ragdolls and will not moult hair all over the house as much as the latter.

If you are an extremely house-proud person, you may find it difficult to accept that your home and furnishings will be 'enhanced' by your kitten's presence, whether that is with his hair, paw prints or claw marks. If you are very fastidious about tidiness, think twice about taking on a kitten as a pet. Kittens love to play, explore and have fun, and will not understand if you shout or disapprove of them for engaging in perfectly natural behaviour.

Pedigree or moggy?

If you would like to get a pedigree kitten you may have to wait some time, and be prepared to travel a considerable distance, particularly if it is one of the more rare breeds or coat patterns. In some cases you may have to wait patiently for between three to six months.

There are pros and cons for owning either a pedigree or a domestic cat of unknown breeding (often referred to as a moggy). There are so many pedigree cats to choose from that there is definitely something to suit everyone's personal tastes and preferences. You can choose from shorthaired cats, longhaired cats and even cats with no hair at all like the hairless Sphynx cat, which some people with allergies find they are able to tolerate. Every colour is available, from chocolates to lilacs, silvers and blue with all the shades in between. Some colours are much rarer than others and if your heart is set on a particular colour you may have to wait longer and pay more than for one of the more common choices. At the end of the day, when it comes to choosing a pedigree rather than a moggy much comes down to budget and personal preference but here are some ideas for you to think about.

- **Cost** – A pedigree kitten can seem expensive (usually several hundred pounds) but breeders have many costs to cover including stud fees, travelling expenses, maintenance of cat accommodation, vet fees, insurance, food, cat litter and, often, the initial vaccinations and microchipping fees. Non-pedigrees or cross-breeds are easier to obtain and less expensive to buy.
- **Family history** – If you buy a pedigree cat you will be able to view his family tree, and know exactly who his parents and grandparents were. You may even be able to see them. This may not be possible with a non-pedigree or cross-breed.
- **Appearance** – When you buy a pedigree kitten you know what it will look like as an adult. You will also have an idea of how it will behave. Non-pedigrees can still make lovely pets but there are no guarantees how they will look as adults, and if the family history is uncertain you will have no clues as to future behaviour traits or health problems.
- **Health** – Some pedigree cats have a genetic predisposition to certain health problems. Ask the breeder whether the kitten you are interested in might possibly be vulnerable to anything and if so be prepared to budget for extra veterinary fees. For example, Persians and some other breeds can be prone to an inherited disease known as polycystic kidney disease (PKD) and you can check whether the kitten's parents have been screened for this.

Generally speaking non-pedigrees are considered to be hardier but those that have had an uncertain start in life, and have not been vaccinated or neutered early on, can also be vulnerable to health problems in later life.
- **Maintenance** – By doing your research you will know whether the breed you are considering is high or low maintenance in terms of grooming and behaviour. Some Oriental breeds, such as Siamese (see Plate 3), are known to be high maintenance emotionally, as they are very active, can be extremely vocal and often get into mischief! Other breeds, such as a Persian, are very placid by nature but are considered

high maintenance because they require rigorous daily grooming to prevent their coats becoming matted. A shorthaired domestic non-pedigree is usually quite low maintenance by comparison, although all cats are individuals and this is not always the case!

Male or female?

Again this is really down to personal preference although male cats are generally larger and heavier, so if you suffer from any physical problems such as arthritis that could make it difficult for you to pick up or handle a large cat, you may be better considering a smaller, lightweight female cat or kitten.

Popular pedigree breeds

According to the Governing Council of the Cat Fancy, the top ten cat breeds in the UK are:

1 British Shorthair
2 Siamese
3 Persian
4 Bengal
5 Burmese
6 Birman
7 Maine Coon
8 Ragdoll
9 Exotic Shorthair
10 Oriental

(These can all be seen in the colour plate section.)

British Shorthair

Renowned for being an intelligent, home-loving cat, the sweet-natured British Shorthair (see Plate 4) is an extremely popular choice of pet. The breed's roots are derived from working cats and their ancestors were brought to Britain by the Romans between the first and fourth centuries. It is thought that the famous grinning Cheshire cat in the Alice in Wonderland story by Lewis Carroll was actually a British Shorthair. The British Shorthair is considered to be one of the hardiest and healthiest of all the pedigree cat breeds. They do love their food, though, and care must be taken to watch their weight. Because the cats have a plush, double layer coat it is very easy to groom and this makes them a low maintenance choice, ideal for busy owners. Males are generally much larger than females. They are very friendly and affectionate cats and are brilliant in a family environment where there are children. They are also usually very good with other animals, including dogs. British Shorthairs are available in a wealth of colours and coat patterns, the most famous and popular of which is solid blue. You can also get them in a delicate cream colour, black, cinnamon and fawn as well as tabby, tortie, spotted, colourpointed and tipped.

Siamese

The beautiful Siamese (see Plate 3), with its sapphire blue eyes, originated from modern-day Thailand (formerly known as Siam) where it was considered to be sacred. In those days the Siamese cats were known as royal points. They were owned exclusively by the royal family and confined to the palace grounds. Siamese are an ancient breed, and are referred to in a manuscript entitled *The Cat Book Poems*, which dates back to 1350. They are livewire bundles of mischief from kittens right through to old age. They are highly intelligent cats, usually very vocal and extremely athletic but can be quite demanding if they think their owners are not paying them enough attention. For this reason Siamese are considered to be high maintenance, although their coats are short, fine and silky making them easy to groom and take care of. In the early years it was unusual to see any variety of colour other than the traditional seal points with its dark brown face, ears, lower legs and tail. However, new colours have been introduced including blue, lilac, chocolate, red, cream, caramel, fawn, cinnamon and apricot points. They are also now available with tortie and tabby markings.

Persian

The glamorous Persian (see Plate 2) is almost as famous for its sweet, placid nature as it is for its luxurious, thick longhair coat. First established over 100 years ago, the look of the Persian has changed considerably since the early days when they had a much longer face than today's breeders aim for. They are very low maintenance in terms of personality and temperament but extremely high maintenance in terms of coat care. Unless they are brushed and combed for at least ten minutes every day the coat will become extremely matted and the cat will look and feel very unhappy. Some breeders recommend that a Persian needs bathing once a month to help keep the coat in good condition. The coat is long and thick, but should not feel too woolly, with a full ruff on the chest which continues down between the front legs and up around the face. They are medium to large cats, and the eyes are large and round and should be set well apart. Because of the shape of their face the tear ducts are slightly distorted, making Persians prone to runny eyes. Persian owners must be prepared to clean the eyes at least once or twice a day with a cotton wool pad dipped in clean, boiled water that has cooled down. The eye colour will either be blue, green, orange or copper, depending on the coat colour. Persian cats are so loving and amiable they make excellent family pets and are very tolerant of children.

Persian breeders have created an almost infinite choice of coat colours. There is the self (a solid colour), available in black, white, blue, red, cream or chocolate. There are the smokes, which have a white undercoat with a coloured overcoat in a whole range of colours including chocolate and lilac torties. The glamorous Chinchilla has a pure white coat that shimmers as silver because of tiny black tips on each hair and they have distinctive green eyes. There are also shaded silvers, Golden Persians, Cameo, Pewter, tabby, tortoiseshell, bi-colours and colour points to choose from!

Bengal

The exotic Bengal (see Plate 5) will appeal to anyone who dreams of owning a pet that has the look of a wild cat and the temperament of a sweet home-loving domestic puss. A cross between a domestic cat and an Asian Leopard, this breed was first created in the USA in the 1970s. Although the distinctive coat is spotted like a leopard, that is where the resemblance ends and they do not have a wild or dangerous streak in their nature. Interestingly, Bengals are reported to share their ancestor's love of water and are said to be highly intelligent. With regard to colours, Bengals are available in a classic brown colour, which can vary in shade to silver-grey or even a light orange. The coat of the stunning marbled Bengal is made up of three colours – brown, black and cream – and there is now also a snow version of the spotted and marbled Bengal. Breeders have recently developed a Silver Bengal, which has a silvery white coat and large black/charcoal rosette style spots making them simply stunning to look at.

Temperamentally they are said to
adapt well to family life, mixing w
pets. They are very loyal and devote
following them from room to room.
readily to being walked on a harness
trained very easily to obey commands and

Bengals are expensive to buy but availability is
cats can weight 6.8–9 kg and females are ligh
at around 4.5–5.5 kg. Because Bengals are so
mischievous it may be better to get two kittens as
other breeds – they can get into all kinds of trouble are
bored and left alone all day.

Burmese

The elegant Burmese (see Plate 6) is renowned for being full of personality and intelligence. They are muscular in build but graceful and sleek as well. They are extremely sociable cats and thrive on company, either human or that of another cat. They really do not enjoy being alone and it is always advisable to keep more than one cat when you have a Burmese, although they can be quite dominant with other breeds.

In 1930, a retired US Navy psychiatrist named Joseph C. Thompson returned from Rangoon in Burma to the USA with a little brown cat called Wong Mau who was to become the foundation queen of the Burmese breed. As a cat breeder, he was convinced that she differed very markedly from the Siamese, but other breeders dismissed Wong Mau as a 'bad Siamese'. Undeterred, Dr Thompson embarked upon a successful breeding programme, initially using a seal point Siamese with Wong Mau and then mating one of the kittens back again. The Burmese was accepted for registration in 1936 but controversy and protests from Siamese breeders resulted in it being withdrawn again. Burmese breeders worked hard to establish the breed and the registration was restored in 1957. Burmese were imported into the UK in 1949 and recognized here in 1952.

Burmese are medium size cats of foreign type and have short, silky coats, which are easy to care for. The original brown Burmese is very popular but they are available in many other colours including blue, chocolate, lilac, red and cream, plus the tortie coat pattern. Their almond eyes are yellow in colour, with a hint of green or orange. Burmese are joyful cats and maintain their kitten like joie-de-vivre long into adulthood. They will take

...keep you entertained all day long (whether ... or not!). It has been noted that Burmese seem to ... enjoy playing retrieval games in which they fetch ...carry a toy that has been thrown for them, in much the same way as a dog.

Birman

The origins of this gorgeous and majestic breed of cat are a little controversial and surrounded in mystery. The myth of the 'Sacred Cat of Burma' comes from its links with temples in Indo-China where it is claimed that the cats were kept as guardians. The name Birman (see Plate 7) derives from the French name for the breed, 'Birmanie' and it is known that French cat lovers kept Birmans in the 1920s. They were first imported to Britain in 1965. They are slightly smaller cats than the Colourpoint Persian or Ragdoll and have a colourpointed coat with white gloves and socks, which extend right up the leg. Birmans have less dense coats than Persians and they look and feel silkier. They are not as high maintenance in terms of coat care as the Persian but regular brushing and combing is still needed to keep it in reasonably good condition.

Breeders say that Birmans make ideal companions, are easy to care for and have wonderful personalities. They are available in a range of 20 different colours and the original seal point is still a firm favourite. You can also get chocolate, red, lilac, tortie and tabby points.

Birmans are quite easy to get hold of, make good family pets and are tolerant of young children and other pets. They are home loving and can live quite happily as indoor cats provided they are given enough mental and physical stimulation to prevent them from becoming bored.

Maine Coon

Maine Coons (see Plate 8) are often described as powerful and imposing semi-longhaired cats but are said to be very well mannered and undemanding, making characterful pets. There is some mystery surrounding the origins of the breed although it is known that the name Maine comes from the state of Maine in the USA. One story is that an English sea captain named Captain Coon, who operated in trading ships in the early days of the colonies, was also a big cat lover. Some of the cats that he took with him on his travels were said to disembark at various ports and breed with the local cats. However, breeders tend to think it is more likely the Maine Coon descended from local house cats that became semi-wild and then developed a heavier body and thicker coat to cope with the harsh climate and life in the forests. They were first imported to the UK in 1983. Although they look like gentle giants and have very thick, heavy coats, which are said to feel as soft as cashmere, they are not as heavy as some of the other breeds. Male Maine Coons weigh around 6–8 kg with females weighing 4–5 kg.

Maine Coons are available in a wide range of colours, the most common being the native brown tabby. Solid and dilute colours such as black, blue and white, red and cream are also available, with tabby coat patterns if desired. Smokes, shaded, bi-colours, and particolours (e.g. blue tortie, silver and white) can also be found. Eyes are full, round and wide apart in all shades of green, gold or copper. Odd or blue eye colours are considered to be permissible in white cats.

They are placid in nature and remain playful into adulthood. They enjoy the great outdoors and often have an affinity to water. Interestingly, it is often observed that when a Maine Coon drinks from his water bowl he will scrape at the surface as if clearing imaginary leaves, which is thought to be a behaviour trait that was inherited from the days when they drank from forest pools.

Ragdolls

Anyone who wants a cat that is a loving companion will adore owning a Ragdoll (see Plate 1) as they tend to follow 'their' people around everywhere and are incredibly sweet natured. Ragdolls were initially bred in California in the 1960s and introduced into the UK in the 1980s. They were named after their tendency to 'flop' like a doll in their owner's arms, although tests have shown that Ragdolls are no more likely to do this than any other loving breed of cat. Myths that the Ragdoll has a lower pain threshold than other cats have also been dismissed and as much care and respect should be given when handling them as any other breed.

Because there is some Birman in the breed's ancestry they are not dissimilar in appearance. Ragdolls have three recognized coat patterns; the colour point, mitted and bi-colour. They are available in all colours and variations of lilac, seal, blue, chocolate, red and cream with solid points, tortie points, tabby points and tortie tabby points, so there are lots to choose from. The colour pointed Ragdoll is still the most popular and is often referred to as 'puss in boots'. Ragolls can grow into massive cats, with the males weighing in at almost 7 kg, so small children and anyone with a physical disability such as arthritis may find them quite heavy to lift. Females tend to be a little less heavy, weighing 4–5 kg. They have beautiful blue eyes, a wedge-shaped face, a long, bushy tail and the coat is medium length, silky and dense. The coat is said to be quite easy to maintain because there is no thick undercoat and they do not moult.

Ragdolls are low maintenance cats, and adore people. They remain inquisitive and playful throughout their lives and can live indoors. Many breeders prefer their kittens to live indoors because they say the breed is not particularly streetwise and would be vulnerable to any traffic. However, Ragdolls would enjoy the company of a playmate if their owners were out at work all day.

Exotic Shorthair

If you are attracted to the look of the Persian breed, but are daunted by the thought of all the grooming involved, the Exotic Shorthair (see Plate 9) may be the cat for you. They are sometimes referred to as the 'easy care' or 'lazy man's Persian' but are affectionate, gentle shorthaired cats. They have a reputation as good family pets, are excellent with children and are considered to be quite hardy, happy to live indoors or venture outside.

The Exotic Shorthair originated in the USA in the 1960s when breeders crossed Persians with American Shorthair is to develop a short-coated Persian type. The breed was developed in the UK in the 1980s and is now well established. Some Exotics can have quite an open face but others have extremely flat faces (referred to as ultras) and this can cause a lot of eye weeping. Potential owners should realize that they will have to work quite hard to keep the eyes clean as part of the grooming routine and the cats may develop eye problems such as conjunctivitis which will require veterinary treatment. Because of the short coat, they are low maintenance in terms of grooming which need only be done once or twice a week. Like its cousin the Persian, the Exotic does have an undercoat and this will become knotted and tangled if it is not combed regularly. They also lose a lot of hair when moulting, so anyone who is fanatically house-proud should bear this in mind.

Exotics are extremely friendly and love sitting with their owners and being cuddled but are not considered to be attention-seeking so can happily live alone, even if their owners have to go out to work during the day. Exotic Shorthairs are large to medium cats and are available in the same colours as the Persian. With over 90 variations of colours and patterns to choose from you will have no difficulty finding something you love.

Oriental

The extrovert, friendly and intelligent Oriental (see Plate 10), which includes Foreign Whites and Havanas, owes much to its flamboyant Siamese cousin. They are certainly not cats for anyone who likes a quiet life and are the very opposite of a couch potato! Life will never be dull with an Oriental or two around but they love company and if left alone can easily become bored and slightly destructive, perhaps by climbing the curtains or clawing the furniture. Owners who are out at work all day would probably be better getting a second Oriental or a Siamese so that they can keep each other entertained.

Developed as a breed in the UK in the 1950s, the Orientals are basically Siamese cats without the traditional Siamese markings and, with the exception of the Foreign White, have intense green eyes rather than the sapphire blue of the Siamese. The coat is short and glossy and they are considered to be low maintenance in terms of grooming. They are often quite fastidious about keeping themselves clean but enjoy the attention of being groomed by their owners. The longhair Oriental (Angora) with its silky coat will require more attention to keep the tangles away. They are considered generally to be quite hardy cats and live into their late teens.

With regard to colours and coat patterns, the choice is almost infinite and whatever your preference, there will certainly be an Oriental to match it. They are fairly easy to obtain although if you want one of the less common colours or coat patterns you may have to wait a while for kittens, or be prepared to travel in order to find one.

Do not forget that your kitten's personality is much more important than the way he looks. Owners who fall in love with their cat's character are likely to forge a deep relationship with them that will last for many years.

One kitten or two?

Although some people think that if they are getting one kitten, having two will not make much difference, they are wrong. You are definitely getting double trouble in terms of veterinary expenses, feeding costs, boarding fees and time for grooming, etc. That said, there is no doubt that two kittens can be a lot of fun, they can really help to entertain each other if you are out at work during the day and will keep each other amused and prevent boredom from setting in. You are also getting two unique kitten personalities that will love you and entertain you for hours on end!

Care should be taken to try to match cat personalities when you are getting two kittens or another cat as a companion for an existing pet. Avoid two extreme personality types, for example two kittens that are over friendly may start to compete for their owner's affections or if they are very shy they may prefer to interact with each other and ignore their owner. It is therefore advisable to get two kittens with what are considered to be 'middle of the road' personalities.

Some breeds tend to settle best with cats of their own type. In particular, because Siamese can be quite territorial and may bully less domineering types such as longhairs, they tend to get on better with other Siamese or cats of their type such as Burmese or Orientals. Although some Siamese breeders advise against keeping two male Siamese together, claiming that they will try to dominate each other and could start spraying, this type of dominant behaviour has been known to occur with other breeds as well.

Some of the more placid, laid-back breeds of cat such as the Ragdoll or Chinchilla may not appreciate the constant attention of one of the other livewire breeds such as a Devon Rex. If you intend to get two kittens of different breeds have a chat with the breeder to ask their opinion on whether they think they are likely to be compatible.

Feral kittens

If you live in a rural area with access to barns or other outhouses, you may like to consider offering a home to one or two feral cats. In the UK the feral cat population is thought to total over 1 million and rescue organizations are always desperate to find good homes for them. Ferals are cats that are untamed and unsocialized and as a result may not be suitable as pets but they can provide a valuable, environmentally friendly pest control service keeping down the mouse population in areas where these are a nuisance, such as the grain store of a riding school or similar establishment.

Feral kittens and some adults can, if given plenty of patience, time and gentle socialization, gradually accept handling from humans and become domestic cats. However, your expectations must be realistic as they are a challenge and should only be taken on by an experienced handler who is prepared to accept failure as some ferals will never trust a human sufficiently to allow themselves to be touched, despite enormous dedication and persistence.

Catching and eating vermin alone will not provide ferals with the balanced diet they need for optimal health so you will still have to feed dry or wet cat food. Feeding them little and often, preferably by hand, will also help to gain trust and form the beginnings of a bond between you. Laying a trail of treats that leads to you can also help to create a positive association.

In addition, feral cats need a warm, safe, draught-free shelter to sleep in and should be provided with medical treatment if needed. Ferals must be neutered to stop them breeding and colonizing another unhappy group of wild cats. Rescue organizations can provide humane traps to help capture and transport feral cats to the vets for treatment.

Sadly, many feral cats are infected with disease such as feline leukaemia, which they have picked up through fighting with other infected cats. It is wise to have any feral cat tested for disease before agreeing to take one on.

Where to get a kitten

If you are thinking of getting a pedigree kitten, the Internet is a useful tool to help you source breeders in your area. The classical section of cat magazines and your local newspaper will be full of advertisements for people who breed cats and dogs. Your library and the notice board at your veterinary surgery may also have information on breeders. Your vet may be able to recommend a reputable breeder who brings their cats in for regular screening and health treatments.

Before deciding on a particular breed, it is advisable to visit some cat shows to observe the cats for yourself. You can also chat with breeders about what these cats are really like to live with, and ask how well they are likely to settle into family life, if they are good with children, or suitable for a working owner, etc.

Once you have spoken to a breeder and confirmed that they have kittens available, arrange to visit them at home. Never be tempted to buy a kitten from a kitten farm where the queen is kept outdoors and the kittens have not been socialized and kept as pets in a happy, home environment. Ask to see the mother and, if possible, the stud cat and assess whether they are kept in clean, comfortable conditions and seem happy and healthy.

Avoid buying a kitten from a pet shop, as you will not have access to his parental history and could be taking on a cat that has come from a kitten farm that may be vulnerable to health and behaviour problems.

Rescue kittens

Rescue organizations and shelters will undoubtedly have kittens and cats that are available for rehoming, although some times of the year are busier than others. Be prepared to undergo quite rigorous home and family assessments and answer some fairly personal and intense questions before you are allowed to take on a kitten. Although potential owners are sometimes offended by the level of questioning they are subjected to, this is done to ensure that a kitten does not end up going to the wrong home and risk being returned some months later. Many organizations have developed a questionnaire to help match the right kitten to the right owner and home. If the kitten has not yet been neutered you will probably be asked to undertake this and may have to accept a home visit a few months later to check that all is well.

Although rescue cats and kittens will be cheaper to buy, you will probably be asked to pay a donation or fee to cover the shelter's costs so that they are able to help more kittens in the future.

Show time!

If you have plenty of money and time available and are passionate about grooming you may like to consider buying a show kitten. Showing can be a fun and sociable pastime, provided you do not take it too seriously and are prepared to accept disappointments with grace and good humour. Show quality kittens will be the very best ones that your breeder has and this will be reflected in the prices they charge. Show quality kittens must be registered with the show sponsor organization, either the Governing Council of the Cat Fancy (GCCF) or Felis Britannica in the UK or the Cat Fanciers Association in the USA.

Kittens and cats should only be shown if they are likely to enjoy the experience and have the right temperament for this.

Show cats are expected to tolerate quite prolonged physical handling and assessments by the judges and then come under the close scrutiny of many spectators as they peer into their cages. They will also undergo a mandatory vet check at the start of the show and if any health problems are noticed they will be disqualified. Some cats enjoy all the attention and fuss, while others find it quite traumatic. If after showing your kitten once or twice he seems to be upset by the experience or dislikes travelling, he is clearly not going to enjoy life as a show cat and you should end his career.

Although breeders sell only their best, top quality kittens for showing, any kittens that do not meet the rigorous standards set by the breed club may be suitable for breeding. Others that are considered below standard (perhaps because of some tiny flaw that is virtually unnoticeable to the inexperienced eye) are sold as pet quality cats. Most breeders will insist that these kittens are neutered as a prerequisite of the sale.

Top Cat Tip

The best show kittens need to be placid but also quite extrovert and natural born show-offs. Judges are looking for a kitten that not only meets the breed standard but also has the 'X-factor'!

Show facts

Kittens are shown between 14 weeks and nine months and even if you do not have a pedigree cat, you may be able to show him in non-pedigree classes if he has the right temperament. Although showing is all about beauty, personality is important too and there are lots of fun classes at local shows such as the cat with the longest whiskers or the cutest face!

There is always a lot of paperwork involved with showing, so allow enough time to complete this. You will need the kitten's GCCF registration or transfer certificate as the entry forms will ask for a lot of information including the cat's name, registration number and details of the sire and dam. You will also need to enclose a cheque to cover the entry fees for the classes you are entering.

The most prestigious shows are championship events. There are also specialist championship shows that cater for a single breed or group. Sanction shows are similar to championship shows without challenge certificates. Exemption shows are smaller and challenge certificates are not awarded, making them ideal for novices as judges often have more time to offer advice. All adult non-pedigree show cats must be neutered and a neuter can only compete in classes for neuters.

Enthusiasts do not show for financial rewards. Prizes are mainly certificates and rosettes, which will be pinned onto the cages after judging, but of course it is a great thrill for a judge to affirm that the kitten you adore is indeed as gorgeous as you thought. However, if you are not lucky enough to win, do not be too disappointed as to an owner, their kitten will always be deserving of first prize!

Equipment

If you intend to show your kitten you will need to purchase some extra equipment for him. Whether he is a pedigree kitten or a non-pedigree he will need:

- A top-opening carrier
- A selection of clean white blankets and towels
- White feed bowl and litter tray
- Supply of cat litter
- Disposal bags
- Water bowl that will not tip over in a cage
- Some white tape or ribbon for the cat's show number (referred to as a 'tally')
- Vaccination certificates
- Box of grooming equipment
- Cleaning equipment, wipes and diluted disinfectant
- Ice pack in hot weather
- Hot water bottles in cold weather.

For more information on showing you can contact the Governing Council of the Cat Fancy or Felis Britannica – see Taking it further on page 147 for details.

Choosing a happy, healthy kitten

CHOOSING A KITTEN.

figure 1 they're all gorgeous, which should you choose?

If you are faced with a litter of adorable non-pedigree kittens it can be difficult and sometimes overwhelming to know which one to choose. To help you decide, consider your own personality, lifestyle, the home you are able to offer and whether you want a kitten that is very extrovert or a more placid laid back individual that will take up less of your time and energy.

Behaviourists advise avoiding a kitten that is hiding in the corner or appears disinterested in his littermates, as he may be too timid for the average owner to enjoy. Similarly, a kitten that is very outgoing and throws itself at you as soon as you enter the room could well be a real handful once you get him home!

Take your time watching the kittens and observe which one is interested in everything, plays happily with the other kittens but is confident enough to come and say hello to you. Ask the breeder when the kittens were last fed, and when they last had a sleep as this could affect how they interact with you on your first meeting. A sleepy kitten is unlikely to want to play very much but later in the day he may be much more lively. It is a good idea to take a friend or another family member with you when you choose your kitten, especially if you have children, so that you can see how well socialized he is and how he responds to different individuals.

Questions to ask the breeder

- When were the kittens born?
- Can you see the mother (and possibly the father)?
- Have the kittens been reared indoors or outside?
- What are their temperaments like?
- Are they used to other pets?
- Have they met lots of different people?
- Are they accustomed to being groomed, handled and having their claws clipped and teeth cleaned?
- Are they going to be high or low maintenance in terms of grooming and care?
- Are they vaccinated and microchipped?
- Do they have any insurance?

Many breeders pass on some free insurance cover to new owners. Pet insurance companies offer this in the hope that new owners will extend the cover when the kitten goes to a new home. It is advisable to accept the insurance cover if it is offered but do your own research into policies before committing to further payments. See Chapter 02 for further information on insuring your cat.

Top to toe health check

When you have found the kitten you think you like the best, pick him up gently, supporting him underneath his bottom and have a good look at him (see Plate 11). In particular, pay attention to:

- **Eyes** – These should be clear and free from any discharge. There should be no sign of a grey-coloured third eyelid, which can indicate health problems.
- **Nose and ears** – Clean and free from any discharge. Be wary if the kitten sneezes frequently or has a runny nose.
- **Teeth** – Your kitten should have a full set of deciduous (baby) teeth. He should have a straight bite and the jaw should be

neither over nor undershot, as these anomalies can make feeding difficult. The gums should be a healthy pink colour.

- **Coat** – Should be clean, and not greasy. There should not be signs of excessive dandruff or little black specks that can indicate the presence of fleas.
- **Bottom** – Clean with no evidence of diarrhoea or worms.

Checklist of paperwork

When you finally agree on the kitten you want you can pay the deposit for him, and ask when you can be allowed to take him home. For a non-pedigree kitten this will probably be between the age of eight and ten weeks, when he has had his first vaccine; pedigree kittens often do not leave the breeder until they are 12–16 weeks old. Do not be disappointed that you cannot take him home straight away, as you will need the time to prepare your home for his arrival and make sure you have all the equipment you need. When choosing a date to bring him home, avoid times when you are likely to be busy at work, or have arranged a family party or scheduled any building work. If possible arrange to bring him home during the week especially if you have children at school. This will give the kitten plenty of time to settle down during the day before the children get back.

On the day you take your kitten home, you should check you are given the following paperwork:

- Vaccination and insurance certificates
- Diet and care sheets
- A written receipt of payment from you
- If he is a pedigree, you need the relevant registration/transfer slip, which you and the breeder complete
- In the UK, if the kitten is registered with the Governing Council of the Cat Fancy (GCCF), you should also be supplied with a copy of the Code of Ethics.

Also make sure you have the breeder's telephone numbers plus an email address in case you have any concerns they might be able to help you with. Most reputable breeders will be happy to answer any queries about their kitten's early days in his new home, so be wary of getting a kitten from a breeder who seems keen to wash their hands of the kitten's welfare once he leaves their establishment.

Did you know?

Early learning

Research shows that the first seven weeks of a kitten's life are the most important in determining how well he adapts to life as a domestic cat. It is during this socialization period that kittens learn to bond with humans. This is why a reputable breeder will take the time to introduce the kittens to as many people and experiences as they can before letting them go to a new home. You can continue this socialization programme as a new owner, introducing your kitten to as many sights and sounds as possible, including vacuum cleaners, hair driers, televisions, music, etc., as well as lots of different adults, children and pets.

02

home time!

In this chapter you will learn:
- how to prepare your home
- about the kitten-friendly garden
- how to keep your kitten healthy.

Once you have reached this exciting stage, there is plenty of work ahead as you prepare everything for your kitten's arrival. One of the first things you need to do is to become registered with a vet. It is essential to do this before your kitten arrives in case you have any problems in the first few days and he needs medical attention.

Finding a vet

If you are not already registered with a veterinary surgery the best way to find one is to ask other cat owners for their recommendations. If you are very lucky there may be a surgery that specializes in caring for cats. Get the telephone number and arrange to visit the surgery and have a chat with the staff. Even if you telephone when the surgery is busy the staff should be polite and offer a time that it is convenient for you to have a look around and see what facilities are available.

Try to find a surgery that is easy for you to get to (you may have to travel there at peak times or even at night if there is an emergency) and where there is plenty of available parking space.

When you arrive your first impression should be that the surgery smells clean and looks tidy and welcoming.

As you enter the reception area the prices of consultations, and various treatments and procedures should be on display and easily visible.

Questions to ask

- Do you have an appointment system?
- Do you have any cat-only clinics?
- How long does each client have with the vet?
- Are there any early morning or evening clinics?
- What happens if my cat is ill out of surgery hours?
- Do you run your own emergency service or is this done by another practice?
- Do you provide free prescriptions?
- When am I expected to pay for treatments?
- Is it ever possible to pay by instalments?

When you have found a vet that you are happy with, it is best to stay with that practice so that only one surgery holds your cat's records and is able to build up a complete health profile for him.

> **Important!**
>
> Cats can react to medicines very differently to other pets, such as dogs, so never be tempted to treat them yourself using human medications. In particular, over-the-counter painkillers such as aspirin and paracetamol can be very dangerous to cats.

Insurance

There is no doubt that emergency veterinary care can be expensive. If your kitten develops health problems or is involved in an accident and requires surgery it can be very stressful to worry about how you are going to find the money to pay for his vet's bills. Investing in some pet insurance is a very good idea and it will help to give you peace of mind. If you have bought a pedigree kitten he may already have some insurance and the company will no doubt hope that you will renew this but do your research first to get the best deal possible for you and your cat. The Internet has made it easier than ever to obtain good value policies and within minutes you should be able to get a quote and if necessary purchase a policy. If you prefer, you can telephone the company and obtain a free quote in this way.

- Pet insurance companies often advertise in the national press, or you can find information leaflets at your veterinary surgery, supermarket or pet discount store.
- Do not be immediately lured into buying a policy just because it advertises special offers and discounts. Take time to read the small print. With a kitten you should not have to worry about cover for an ongoing condition, but this is something you will need to take into account with an older cat. Find out what the age limit is for the policy or whether it offers life cover for your cat.
- Check if the policy will cover consultations with a pet behaviour counsellor or any complementary therapies such as homeopathy or acupuncture. If you intend to travel with your cat, check that the policy will cover any treatment he may need while you are overseas.
- You can also get insurance to cover the costs of advertising if your kitten goes missing, and to offer a reward to help get him safely home again.
- It is also worth getting a policy that covers for accidental damage and third party liability costs.

- The other important thing to check with any insurance policy is the excess fee you are expected to pay. Be wary of companies that state this will be a percentage of the bill rather than a set fee – 10 per cent of a bill that has run into thousands of pounds can be significant.

Compare several policies and then choose the one that offers the most cover for vet's fees (this varies considerably), has the lowest excess (i.e. how much you are expected to pay), no age limit and preferably life cover, with cover for some alternative treatments including behaviour, a low exclusion period (where a pet may be excluded from cover for an existing illness) and reasonable monthly premiums.

> **Top Cat Tip**
>
> Insuring your cat is one of the best ways to avoid having to pay large vet's bills.

Time to go shopping!

Now that you have found a vet and sorted out your insurance, it is time to give some thought to what else you will need to buy for your kitten.

The first thing on your shopping list should be a strong, secure pet carrier that you can bring your kitten home in and use at later dates to transport him to the vet's and boarding establishments. If you are planning to travel with your pet it is essential to get one that is airline approved.

> **Top Cat Tip**
>
> Check out the advertisements in local newspapers or the notice board of your vet's surgery to see if anyone is advertising a second-hand carrier for sale. Once thoroughly cleaned, this can be a cost-effective way of making your cat carrier purchase.

> **Top Cat Tip**
>
> Second-hand child stair gates are also useful for keeping your kitten confined to one room of your house. It can also be used to keep other pets away from your kitten during the early introductory stages.

Shopping list essentials

- **Food and water bowls** and a non-slip mat to stand them on.
- **Kitten food** – Ask the breeder what brand of food the kitten is being fed and stock up on this for the first few weeks of your kitten's new life.
- **Flea comb and grooming brushes** – Your breeder or vet will be able to recommend those are most suitable for your kitten's coat type.
- **Bed** – There are many fancy cat beds available but to be honest, a plastic crate or a cardboard box with a cushion and blanket will be perfectly adequate for the first few weeks.
- **Litter tray and cat litter** – Check which type the breeder used and use a similar tray and the same litter for the first few weeks. Some cats prefer the privacy of a covered litter tray but a simple plastic tray, lined with newspaper or tray liner, will suffice.
- **Litter picker** – An implement to remove soiled litter and faeces from the tray.
- **Rubber gloves** – Essential when handling soiled cat litter.
- **Toys** – You do not have to spend a fortune on kitten toys as it is often the simplest ones that he will like best. Scrunched up paper, a ping-pong ball or a ball of crushed silver paper is ideal. However, you can buy more expensive, interactive toys that dispense treats when moved, or toys that will encourage the kitten's instinct for hunting.
- **Scratch posts** – Essential so that your kitten can sharpen his claws on something other than your furniture!

Did you know?

Cats prefer to stretch up and scratch vertically rather than horizontally. Cats are creatures of habit and do not like their scratching posts to be moved around, possibly because they leave a scent mark from their footpads, to alert other cats that they live here. This helps to make them feel secure.

Other items

As your kitten grows you might like to invest in some extra bits and pieces to help enrich his environment and keep him happy. These items can include:

- **Collar** – Avoid putting one on your kitten until he is at least six months old and then check the fit regularly to ensure it continues to be the right size. Some collars contain magnets for access to cat flaps but all collars must have a safety section that snaps open easily if the cat becomes tangled up on something such as the branch of a tree.
- **Cat flap** – Once your kitten has been vaccinated you may like him to enjoy more independence and consider having a cat flap fitted.
- **Outdoor cat run** – This can be very useful if you want to control his access to the great outdoors, particularly if you live close to a busy road. There are many available from commercial pet stores or garden centres but you can also commission a joiner to make one for you.
- **Activity centre** – You can buy climbing frames for cats with different levels, hiding places and toys attached, all designed to help keep your cat entertained and exercised throughout the day.

Top Cat Tip

Invest in a folder or box file to put all your cat's paperwork in and keep it in a safe place. Store his vaccination and pedigree certificates in there, as well as information from your vet or boarding establishment and some recent photographs that you can use on posters in case he ever goes missing.

Grooming kit

Your grooming kit should include:

- Flea comb and wide-tooth metal comb
- Soft bristle brush or slicker brush to remove long hair
- Claw clippers
- Small bowl of tepid water
- Cotton wool balls
- White towel or sheet

- Teeth cleaning products
- Round-ended scissors.

You can also buy a grooming mitt or chamois leather to give a gloss to the coat of shorthaired cats and some unscented talcum powder to help clean and comb through the coat of a long haired cat.

If you groom regularly and make the sessions short and enjoyable your cat will associate this as quality time and an entirely pleasurable experience. Grooming will help to keep his coat clean, tangle-free, improve circulation and enable you to check for any lumps, bumps or injuries that he may have sustained. It is also an excellent opportunity for the two of you to bond and develop trust in each other.

How often should you groom?

- Shorthair cats require weekly grooming.
- Semi-longhairs require grooming two to three times a week.
- Longhair cats require grooming every day.

Preparing for home time!

A few days before your kitten arrives you will need to look at your home room by room and try to create a kitten-proof environment. This is also a great opportunity to ask everyone else in the family to tidy up and de-clutter! As your kitten grows in size and confidence he will love to explore your home so pack away any particularly valuable or fragile ornaments that he might accidentally knock over.

Have a look around each room and see if there are any areas that are small enough for a curious, squirmy kitten to squeeze underneath but have trouble getting back out from. Try to block these areas with furniture or pieces of wood until he gets bigger.

- The kitchen or laundry room is full of potentially dangerous appliances for your kitten so stick labels on the doors of washing machines, tumble driers, dishwashers and ovens, urging everyone in the house to check inside before they close the doors or turn things on. These dark, warm places can look very inviting to a tired kitten who is seeking somewhere to have a snooze!
- Put locks on cupboards and store away household chemicals and medicines.

- Relocate rubbish bins outside in the garage or invest in a tall bin with a fixed lid rather than a swing lid that a kitten can grab on to and fall inside.
- Tidy away anything that contains small, potentially dangerous items such as a sewing box with pins and needles.
- Put a fireguard against open fireplaces to stop your kitten going up the chimney.
- Place indoor plants and vases of flowers safely out of your kitten's reach.
- This is a great opportunity to educate everyone to become disciplined about putting the toilet seat down! Put notices up in this regard if necessary.
- Invest in cable tidiers or tape up any loose, trailing wires that are behind the television or stereo unit.
- Store away plastic bags, as kittens love to play inside them but can easily suffocate.

Did you know?

Like people, cats can be affected by passive smoking, so make a date in your diary to give up before your kitten arrives and encourage any other smokers in the house to do the same. Researchers in the USA have discovered that cats living in homes with people who smoke are more than twice as likely to develop feline lymphoma cancer.

When your kitten first arrives home, it may be best to limit his access to one room until he settles down, particularly if you have other pets. This will allow you to supervise the kitten and allow him to confidently explore in a safe environment without becoming overwhelmed by too many new sights and smells. The kitchen is probably not the ideal place to choose as there is always a lot going on and there are too many places he can crawl under and get stuck.

When you have chosen a room for him, put his bed in a corner and place his food and water bowls close by, where he can easily find them. Make sure the windows and doors are closed before you let him out of his carrier.

When choosing somewhere to put his litter tray, do not place it too close to his food bowls as this could deter him from using it. Put it somewhere that is easily accessible but relatively quiet, not in a high traffic area next to the door. Show him where the litter tray is as soon as he arrives and put him on it after every meal, giving him lots of verbal praise and encouragement every time he uses it. The chances are your kitten will already be house-trained, but you will help him by using the same cat litter as the breeder or shelter that he came from, so that as much as possible seems familiar to him. Some cats are very sensitive to change, and may find a new litter too gritty, soft or clumpy for them to use because it sticks into their pads. Make any changes to the cat litter you use very gradually over the next few weeks.

> **Top Cat Tip**
>
> To help your kitten settle down, take a blanket or towel along to the breeder a few days before you are due to bring him home. Ask the breeder to put this in his bed and then bring the 'comfort blanket' home with the kitten. When you get home, place the blanket in his new bed and the familiar smells will help to reassure and relax him.

Early days

The first few days in his new home can be a very stressful time for a kitten, even though it is always very exciting for everyone else in the family. Hopefully all the preparations you have made beforehand and the timing of his arrival will ensure you have plenty of time available to help him settle in quickly.

Talk to any children in the family and explain that your kitten may be missing his brothers and sisters and feeling rather worried at first. Ask them to respect the time he needs to sleep and to always handle him gently and with care. It is important for children to understand that the kitten is not a toy and they should not be encouraged to carry him around everywhere but rather to sit down so that the kitten comes to investigate them. Give children some treats to offer the kitten, so that he associates them with fun and learns to come when he is called. Treats do not necessarily have to be food, they can be toys and interactive games that your kitten will enjoy playing.

> **Top Cat Tip**
>
> Invest in one or two new videos or DVDs that you can put on to help take your children's attention away from the kitten before he becomes too tired or stressed.

Name games

If you have not already decided on a name for your kitten, now is the time to do so! Choose something that is easy to say and that you will not be embarrassed to shout out loud if he ever goes missing in the garden. In general, the fashion for cat names seems to be swaying towards more human names such as Charlie or Jack rather than descriptive ones such as Misty or Smudge. When choosing a name, remember that your choice may influence whether people react positively or negatively to him. It would not be fair to make him the subject of ridicule.

Interestingly, in his 1939 poem 'The Naming of Cats', *T. S. Eliot* claims cats actually have three names; an everyday name such as Peter, a fancier one for special occasions such as Admetus and, most importantly, a secret name that we humans will never be allowed to know!

> And that is the name that you will never guess;
> The name that no human research can discover –
> But THE CAT HIMSELF KNOWS, and will never confess.

If you need inspiration to help you choose a name for your cat, type in a search on the Internet and you will discover that entire websites have been devoted to the subject.

Did you know?

When you choose a name for your cat you could be revealing more about yourself than you realize! Psychologists believe that in naming their pets people can sometimes subconsciously identify their alteregos (that part of themselves they normally keep hidden). So a very nervous person might choose an aggressive sounding name such as Rambo or Dynamite and someone who is extrovert and a bodybuilding enthusiast might choose a name like Tina Ballerina!

Ground rules

As soon as your kitten arrives home be consistent with any ground rules that you want him to adhere to. For example, discourage him from jumping or climbing up onto work surfaces or furniture, stealing titbits, clawing at the curtains or scratching chairs. For hygiene reasons it is important not to allow your kitten to lick anyone's face. Ensure everyone in the house is aware of what the rules are as it will be very confusing for the kitten if you do not allow him on the sofa but your partner thinks it is a great idea!

Decide where you want the kitten to sleep at night and stick to it. It is not fair to allow him on your bed as a kitten and then decide when he is a fully-grown cat that he is not allowed on there. Give him his own comfy bed and on the first few nights put his comfort blanket in and a well-covered hot water bottle to remind him of mum.

Discourage unwanted behaviour by saying 'no' in a firm voice and lifting him down or away from the furniture. Try using a different, higher-toned voice to give verbal praise and approval for behaviour that you are keen to encourage, such as using the litter tray.

Put your kitten on his litter tray after every meal and every time he wakes up after a nap. If he has an accident, do not get cross with him, simply clean the mess up thoroughly to discourage him from returning to the same spot. Use a non-biological detergent that does not contain ammonia or chlorine, as these are constituents of urine and may attract him back to the area.

Introducing other pets

The key to successfully introducing your kitten to other pets such as cats, dogs or rabbits is to prepare carefully and always take things very slowly. Do not allow them to be left together unsupervised until you are completely confident there will not be a problem.

If you have confined your kitten to one room for a few days, his smell will have pervaded other areas of the house so there will be some familiarity before the pets actually meet. You can also try to bring a positive association with the kitten's smell by gently wiping his face onto a clean flannel and then placing some tasty treats on the cloth for your other pet to find. Extend this further by swapping bedding and toys.

Put your kitten into his carrier for the first introduction so that the existing pets can investigate safely without risk of injury. There may be some hissing and spitting at first but try to ignore this as much as possible and keep any intervention to a minimum. Avoid shouting at or scolding any of the pets as this will make the experience very negative and spoil the introductory process.

If you have an indoor crate this is an ideal way to introduce your kitten to new pets, particularly dogs. Put the kitten into the crate and, with the dog on a lead, allow him to approach and sniff, praising him for behaving well and trying to ignore growling or jumping up. If the dog exhibits aggression, remove him from the situation and try again later.

Try putting some food down next to the carrier and feeding the dog, then placing the dog into the carrier and the kitten on the outside so that he can explore safely. The next time try feeding the two pets together, although one is still in the carrier and the other outside.

Continue to introduce the pets gradually and pay just as much attention to existing pets as always so that they do not feel threatened, insecure or usurped by the newcomer. It is important to disrupt their routine as little as possible. The introductory process can take several weeks but with patience and time, all the pets in your family should integrate with each other, so that they at least tolerate each other although some go on to develop quite close relationships. If you do experience severe problems or things fail to settle down, contact your vet for further advice.

Top Cat Tip

Never be tempted to hurry the process along after a few days by locking the cats in a room together 'to let them sort it out between themselves'. Forcing social contact in this way can be quite traumatic for the cats as well as potentially dangerous.

Kitten behaviour

You will enjoy spending time with your kitten, learning about his personality, the things he likes, what makes him nervous and what reassures him. Taking time to learn what is normal behaviour in your kitten is also very valuable as it will help you to recognize when he is feeling ill or distressed. Most behaviour problems such as toileting indoors are the result of stress so the more effort an owner makes to understand what makes their cat tick, the better equipped they will be to deal with problems before they get too serious. All kittens will vary in temperament and behaviour but there are a few things you can expect to see in all kittens. These include:

- **Sleeping** – Your new kitten will spend 16–18 hours a day sleeping, and this is considered to be entirely normal behaviour for a growing cat.

- **Play** – When he is not asleep your kitten should be keen to play and explore his new environment very enthusiastically. Kittens use play-fighting to develop their hunting skills but will not hiss or spit as in a real fight. If your kitten rolls over onto his back and exposes his stomach this is a sign of submission and not something that would happen in a real fight. After a bout of energetic play he will probably become tired very quickly and flop down suddenly, or he may decide he's hungry and start demanding food!

- **Eating** – Kittens only have tiny stomachs and cannot eat large volumes of food. For this reason they should be fed small meals, five times a day to start with, which can be reduced to twice a day by the age of six months.

- **Drinking** – Ensure your kitten has access to fresh water at all times but do not worry if he does not appear to be drinking very often. Cats are descended from the African Wild Cat, *Felix sylvestris lybica*, and have therefore adapted physically and biochemically to survive in semi-desert conditions. If a cat suddenly seems to be excessively thirsty this can indicate a health problem such as kidney disease, diabetes or an overactive thyroid gland.

- **Watching** – Your kitten's eyes will change colour from baby blue to his adult colour by the time he is three months old. Because cats are natural hunters and sunset and dawn are their most active times, their eyes are cleverly designed to be most effective during these periods. When your kitten plays you may notice that the pupils of his eyes open up considerably so that his eyes appear huge. In bright sunshine however the pupil closes to an almost horizontal slit, and this impairs their vision.

- **Listening** – Your kitten will spend a lot of time listening to what is going on and trying to work out what all the different sounds mean. You may notice him putting his head to one side when he is trying to interpret various noises. He uses over 32 different muscles in order to hear!

Did you know?

It is thought that cats can see up to eight times better than humans in the dark. However, they see fewer colours than we do and are unable to differentiate between reds, which merge into a grey or black. Your kitten will be much more interested in the shape of an object, the shadow it makes and how it moves, rather than the colour of it.

Body language

You can learn a lot about your kitten by the body language he uses to communicate with you. Here are some examples of what you might see:

- **Kneading** – Small kittens often knead their paws either on their owners or a blanket. This reminds them of kneading mum to stimulate milk production and is something they find comforting, as their purring will probably tell you!

- **Leg weaving** – Your kitten may weave himself in and out of your legs, rubbing his face around them as he does so. This is natural marking behaviour and he is covering you with pheromones so that you are a recognizable part of his group. Do not worry, as these pheromones are odourless and invisible! This behaviour often results in the owner petting the cat or picking him up, so he may do this as an attention-seeking activity to initiate contact.

- **The alley cat strut** – If your kitten leaps around with an arched back and his fur standing on end, it often means he wants you to come and play with him. In older cats, however, it usually means the opposite and is a warning to leave them alone, particularly if accompanied by growling and staring.

figure 2 the alley cat strut – an invitation to play or a warning to stay away!

- **Tail wagging** – Usually means there is something very exciting going on, and your kitten would dearly love to pounce on it and find out more!
- **Wide eyes** – It takes less than one second for an excited or frightened cat to expand his pupils up to five times their previous size. He does this to help him see better and assess the situation.
- **Eye contact** – A cat that is curious or very alert will open his eyes wide. If your cat's eyes are half closed this signals that he is feeling very relaxed and trusting.
- **Flehming** – If you notice that your cat suddenly pauses and appears to be sneering, with his upper lips drawn back and his mouth slightly open, he will actually be trying to savour the smell of another cat. This is referred to as the 'Flehmen response' and usually occurs when a male picks up the scent of urine of a female cat on heat. However, it may also occur if a cat notices a new smell in the home. A tiny structure on the roof of the cat's mouth, known as the Jacobsen's organ, is extremely sensitive to airborne chemicals and maximizes the strength of the smell.

Indoors or out?

All kittens should be kept indoors until their vaccination programme has been completed, so they can avoid catching any nasty diseases living in the garden soil or meeting up with any stray unvaccinated cats that may decide to pay them a visit. For various reasons some owners decide never to allow their cats outdoors and, if this is your intention, you need to think carefully whether you are able to offer an environment that will ensure your cat remains happy.

Reasons to keep an indoor cat include:

- Proximity to a busy road
- Living in a high rise apartment
- Illness or disability (such as a cat that is blind or deaf)
- Fear of airgun attacks
- Risk of theft
- Cat-hating neighbours
- To keep the cat cleaner and the coat tangle free.

It is not a natural life for a cat to live indoors and they are more likely to develop behaviour problems. There is also some scientific evidence that increased stress levels experienced by indoor cats makes them more at risk of developing thyroid and bladder problems.

If a cat is in good health and already used to the outdoor life it will be much more difficult for him to accept the confines of indoor living, and it would be cruel to expect him to do so.

Pedigree cats are often kept as indoor pets but some of them are more attention seeking and higher maintenance than others. In general, the longhair cats such as Persians and Chinchillas or the Ragdoll have very placid personalities and are quite happy to live the indoor life without demanding too much attention from their owners. However, cats from the Oriental group such as Siamese or Burmese can quickly become bored if they are not provided with sufficient entertainment. Left unaddressed this boredom can manifest itself in behaviour problems or some form of compulsive disorder such as pica (where cats eat non-nutritional items such as wool) or excessive licking.

If you are out at work all day it is always kinder to have two cats or kittens rather than leave your cat without any company. Two cats or kittens can entertain each other and provide the companionship they need. Introducing a new cat into the family can sometimes be problematic so make life easier for yourself by getting the two kittens together.

There are lots of things you can do to make your cat's indoor life as rich as possible. With the absence of trees and fences to climb, ensure he has plenty of high places to clamber onto and use as a safe vantage point. If you have a multi-cat household, each cat will need access to what he considers a 'safe' area that he can retreat to, such as behind the sofa, on top of an activity centre or bookcase. Clear these areas of any breakable object you are especially fond of, to avoid accidents.

Playing with your cat is always a pleasure but for indoor cats it must be an essential part of daily life. Schedule two or three ten-minute sessions of interactive play to help keep him mentally and physically stimulated. In particular, hunter type play is important, as he will be denied this activity in reality and may find this very frustrating.

Indoor cats will appreciate you growing a window box of grass or catnip for them to nibble on. It is thought that nibbling grass may help cats to regurgitate hair-balls, and some cats certainly seem to be very fond of eating natural vegetation.

Indoor cats can be more at risk of obesity, particularly if they have free access to supplies of dried cat food. Keep an eye on your cat's weight and put him on a restricted calorie diet if necessary, as well as increasing his levels of physical activity. For more tips on how to help an obsese cat drop a collar size see Chapter 04.

As well as providing lots of play areas, retreats and access to windows that he can look out of, ensure your house is cat-proof so that you are not worrying that he will escape the minute your back is turned. Putting mesh up at a window can help.

If possible, allow your cat to have some restricted access to the outdoors, perhaps by some accompanied trips into the garden or by erecting an outdoor run (see Plate 12). This will really help to enhance his life as it will give him a complete change of scenery plus the feeling of fresh air and sunshine. If trained from an early age, some cats will learn to walk on a harness and can enjoy walking with their owners.

Top Cat Tip

Your cat will appreciate the noise of a radio playing during the day when you are out at work. You can even buy special videos and computer screen savers featuring wildlife that have been designed specifically for the entertainment of cats!

The kitten-friendly garden

Once his vaccinations are complete your kitten will be able to start exploring the great outdoors. This will bring a whole new dimension to his world, as he experiences the joys of creeping in long grass, chasing leaves and paddling through a water feature. Although cats are sometimes considered unwelcome visitors to a garden, even professional gardeners keep cats and with a little thought and careful planning there is no reason why you cannot enjoy both your cat and your garden.

Before you let him outside do a thorough check to make sure that fencing is secure and if necessary put gates up to stop him escaping and prevent other animals such as dogs or foxes from coming in.

There are lots of plants that your cat will enjoy, such as the aromatic catnip (*Nepeta cataria*), and if you plant this in an area you have designated for him to play in it will help to keep him away from your other more delicate plants.

Another feline favourite is cat thyme (*Teucrium marum*), and the herb valerian (*Valeriana officinalis*), which sends them wild with delight.

If you have enough space consider planting a clump of bamboo, which is available in many sizes and varieties. Visit your garden centre for advice on what will best suit your plot of land. Not only do cats enjoy wandering through the bamboo jungle, they also like to sleep on the dry leaf matter and watch the amazing shapes and shadows that these plants make.

Did you know?

Your cat will occasionally enjoy chewing on some grass and even if you do not allow him outdoors it is worth growing some for him in a seed tray or window box.

Top Cat Tip

Some pesticides are toxic to cats, so check labelling carefully before applying and do not allow your cat or other pets outside for several hours after spraying.

Sun, shade and water

The three essential items your cat needs outdoors are a nice sunny area where he can relax and have a sleep, shaded areas to retreat to in hot weather and access to fresh water. Anything else is a bonus! However, he will appreciate some tall grasses to hide in, a raised platform area that he can sit on and observe what the rest of the world is doing, plus a comfy garden trug with a blanket or an outdoor cat bed to snooze in. Tree trunks to sharpen his claws on are a good idea, and a patch of short, cool grass to roll on will be greatly enjoyed.

Toilet area

To stop your kitten from using any random area of the garden as a toilet, designate a place for him to go, perhaps by providing a mound of freshly dug soil or sand, which you can keep clean. Take the kitten to this area regularly and praise him when he uses it. Cats are naturally fastidious about hygiene and will not like to use a toilet area that is close to where they play or sleep so locate it in a quiet, private area, perhaps screened by some large shrubs.

Use plenty of ground cover planting on borders so that the surface of the soil is not visible, and this will help to deter the cat from using it as a toilet area. Some gardeners report that using cocoa-shell mulch on the borders also helps to act as a deterrent for cats. Avoid putting down prickly cuttings or pine needles to keep your cat off borders and seedbeds as they may get stuck in his pads and become infected. Positioning a series of short sticks into the ground will help deter him from using the area as a toilet.

Did you know?

Cats will use their faeces to mark what they consider to be their territory. When they feel their territory is being threatened (and this applies to indoor cats as well), they will often leave droppings uncovered, rather than bury them.

Toxic plants

Some varieties of plant are poisonous to cats if they decide to eat them. Some members of the lily family (*Lilium spp.*) including the Easter lily, Glory lily, Asiatic lilies, tiger lily and devil lily/Japanese show lily can result in feline kidney failure. All parts of these plants are toxic to cats and can also have an affect on other pets.

Plants to avoid include:

- Angel's trumpets
- Autumn crocus
- Bluebell
- Burning bush
- Castor oil plant
- Clematis
- Dumb cane
- False Hellebore
- Foxglove

- Laburnum/golden chain
- Lily of the valley
- Oleander
- Rhubarb
- Yew.

Water features

Ponds and kittens are not a good combination but they will certainly appreciate a water feature such as a pebble fountain. Some cats are fascinated by water and will paddle around in it and flick it with their paws. Many of them will enjoy drinking from these, so be wary of adding any chemicals that may be poisonous to them.

Top Cat Tip

Water butts or tanks can be a source of great fascination to cats but are extremely dangerous to them if they climb up and fall in but are unable to get out again. Ensure that these are securely covered with a lid at all times.

Wildlife watch

It is possible to feed birds if you have a cat but take care where you position the feeders and avoid hanging them from sheltered trees where cats can hide and launch themselves. Putting a wire mesh tree collar around the trunk of trees can help deter your cat from climbing up them. Instead, put bird tables in open areas on high poles where they can easily be seen and birds can make a quick escape. It is best to keep cats indoors in the early morning and at dusk when birds are likely to want to feed and flock.

First time out

The first time your kitten goes outside, make sure it is just before he is due to be fed. When you want him to come inside again, rattle a box of biscuits and give him a few special treats to encourage him to come to you whenever he is called. Never shout at a cat for not coming to you, the trick is to try to make yourself much more interesting than anything else he may be doing. High value treats and lots of enthusiastic verbal praise are the best ways to achieve this.

Always supervise your kitten's first few outings to ensure he does not decide to climb a tree and get stuck, and so that you can encourage him if he seems afraid of something. Play a game with him, perhaps twitching a twig for him to try and catch or rolling a ball along for him to chase. Make his time in the garden a really positive experience that he learns to enjoy.

Wide range

According to research, a male cat's range (i.e. the area he normally inhabits) is anything from three to ten times more than a female cat, and he will be much more likely to leave the delights of your garden and enjoy a stroll through a few others. A female cat is generally happier to stay in her own and perhaps part of next-door's garden. Do not forget, cats regard these areas as their territory and will not respect human boundaries! It has been observed that cats in rural areas have larger ranges than cats that live in outer surburbia, while cats that live in densely populated inner surburban areas have much smaller ranges.

Top Cat Tip

By making your garden as secure and interesting as possible you will help to decrease the risk of your cat wandering off into other people's gardens.

Air gun alert

Animal welfare charities estimate that thousands of cats are injured or killed by air gun pellets each year. Although dogs and other pets are also shot, cats appear to be particularly vulnerable to accidental and often deliberate attacks. Unfortunately, shotgun injuries are not always obvious and a cat can suffer tremendous pain before anyone realizes there is a problem. It has been known for an owner to take their cat to the vet simply because they have noticed a loss of appetite and perhaps the cat seems to dislike being handled. It is only when the vet examines and X-rays the cat that the problem comes to light. Surgery is often required to remove the pellet (depending on where it is lodged), if left in situ it could cause permanent paralysis. Vets advise owners to be vigilant when examining their cats, particularly during the summer months when more cats are out and about in the evenings. Small entry wounds are often buried in the fur and an air gun wound is about 1–2 mm in diameter and circular in shape. It is often confused with a cat bite injury.

Cat runs

Investing in an outdoor cat run (see Plate 12) or enclosure is a very useful thing to do, particularly if you are out at work or want to visit friends for the day. There are many available from specialist pet shops and garden centres, or you can commission a competent joiner to make one for you.

To create the perfect home, the run needs to have prefabricated wired panels around each side, a pitched roof for drainage and a secure lockable door. There needs to be a separate warm, draught-free shelter inside that the cat can retreat to, preferably high up with access from a ladder so that the cat can have a good vantage point of the surrounding area. You can also plant some shade-loving evergreens inside, either directly into the ground or in pots to provide alternative shelter and a hiding place. Ensure that any plants you select are not toxic to cats.

Ideally, have a combination of floorings inside the run, such as timber decking, concrete slabs and a gravel area. Place a covered litter tray inside the enclosure and clean this out regularly.

Use your imagination and put lots of toys, tunnels and treats inside for your cat to find so that he really enjoys being inside his outdoor den.

Top Cat Tip

Do not forget to put down bowls of fresh clean water each time the cat uses the enclosure.

Your kitten's health

As soon as you can, make an appointment for your vet to examine your kitten and give him a clean bill of health. Your vet's examination will include weighing him, listening to his heart and lungs, checking his teeth and gums, looking at his eyes and ears, feeling the abdomen for any lumps and bumps and checking his coat for signs of fleas or skin problems. He will also check his vaccination status and if necessary give him his first injection or any boosters that are required. Vaccinations help to give the kitten immunity against some very nasty and potentially fatal diseases. Even indoor cats can be at risk of encountering another unvaccinated cat if they escape. For more information on what vaccines are considered to be essential to your kitten's health and wellbeing, see Chapter 06.

Use the opportunity to ask questions about any aspects of kitten care that you feel uncertain about, such as feeding, grooming or introductions to other pets.

Taking your kitten to the surgery early on in his life gives him the chance to meet the vet and get used to being handled and examined by him. Try to make the experience as stress-free as possible and act as calmly and normally as you can so that the kitten does not pick up on any anxiety from you and think there is something to worry about.

Top Cat Tip

It is a good idea to accustom your kitten to be relaxed about going into and out of his carrier so that he does not always associate it with something stressful. Leave the carrier out at home, and put a few treats and toys in there to encourage the kitten to go inside. Play and pet him in the carrier for a few minutes and then give him a treat and take him out again. Spending time doing this will save you a lot of time in the future, as any owner whose cat has gone into hiding as soon as the carrier comes out will tell you!

Staying healthy

When you groom your kitten it is a great opportunity to give him a quick health check. Take into account your kitten's normal behaviour, appetite and water consumption to assess whether he is feeling happy and well. The best way to maintain optimum health is to:

- Worm him regularly
- Treat him for fleas
- Get him neutered
- Keep his vaccinations up to date
- Feed him a balanced diet of cat food
- Maintain his proper body weight
- Provide him with exercise and mental stimulation
- Take him for an annual check-up.

Taking your cat to the vet once a year for a check-up is important because although it can be easy to spot if he has been obviously injured, some cats can be very stalwart about enduring pain, discomfort and quite major health problems. Long-term chronic problems such as arthritis may go undetected for some time if your vet does not examine him.

Common health problems in kittens

Fleas

Flea infestation is by far the most common problem vets are likely to see in cats of all ages. Contemporary living and centrally heated homes mean that there is no longer a single season for flea infestations and cats are vulnerable to these all year. This means that owners are also vulnerable as fleas are not choosy who or what they bite!

Fleas are ectoparasites, which means they live outside the body of an animal and survive by feeding on the blood of their 'host' animal. There are many different species but they all transmit bacteria and can cause skin irritation, infection, hair loss, discomfort and a condition known as flea allergy dermatitis.

There are many treatments available including collars, sprays, foams and tablets but some of the most effective at killing fleas are available from your vet. Although more expensive than over-the-counter treatments they are considered to be very safe, as well as effective.

Spot-on applicators are quickly and easily applied between the cat's shoulder blades and one dose usually lasts about a month. Some flea products are also known to control roundworms and ear mite infestations. Always check the labelling to ensure that your kitten is old enough to start the treatment.

Has your kitten got fleas?

If your kitten has thick or dark hair it can be difficult to tell whether he has fleas just by looking at him. The easiest way to check is by grooming him. Stand the kitten on a clean white sheet or cloth and thoroughly work through the coat with a flea comb, starting at the head and working towards the tail. If you see any little dark specks on the comb or sheet it could indicate a problem with flea infestation. Flea dirt contains congealed blood, which will dilute to a pinkish colour if placed on a damp piece of cotton wool, so this is a good way of double-checking. Do not panic if you find fleas on your kitten, they are very common and not a sign that he or your home is dirty!

> **Top Cat Tip**
>
> Reduce the risk of toxic reaction by avoiding using any flea products that contain organophosphate ingredients and dispose of all packaging carefully. If you suspect your kitten is having an allergic reaction to a flea product, contact your vet immediately.

Alternative flea treatments

A wide range of alternative flea treatments using natural ingredients is available but it is important to understand that these products will repel fleas rather than kill them and are therefore not as effective. Natural flea repellent collars contain herbs and various essential oils such as lavender, cedarwood, citronella or rosemary. You can also buy shampoos and rinses to bathe the cat and his bedding in.

Some owners have reported success by feeding garlic supplements or adding a quarter teaspoon of cider vinegar into their cat's food. Apparently these treatments are supposed to make the cat's blood less taste less attractive to fleas.

> **Top Cat Tip**
>
> Fleas can live in carpets and your cat's bedding, so it is important to treat your home with insecticides as well. Your vet may be able to supply you with some effective treatments that will clear your home of infestation.

How to prevent flea infestation

- The best way to prevent your cat or kitten from becoming infested with fleas is to comb him regularly with a special flea comb and give a monthly flea treatment.
- Vacuum your carpets thoroughly and steam clean them if infestation is suspected.
- If your kitten has fleas, always treat your home as well as any other pets and their bedding.

Did you know?

- A flea is capable of jumping six feet into the air and can leap from one pet to another in a household. They can remain dormant for up to two years, surviving quite happily in carpets and soft furnishings just biding their time until a tasty victim walks past!
- Within two days of feeding on your little kitten, a female flea will start producing up to 50 eggs a day.

Worms

Kittens can be infected with roundworms, which they have picked up through their mother's milk. If this is the case your kitten will definitely not be looking bright-eyed and healthy, instead he will be small, sickly and have a pot-belly. Roundworms are sometimes vomited and resemble coiled elastic bands. Treatments to eliminate these parasites are available from your vet.

Other worms to look out for are tapeworms, which resemble grains of rice in appearance and are visible when stuck to the fur or the skin around the kitten's bottom. Cat fleas can carry the larval stage of tapeworm, so treating for these can help prevent infestation with tapeworms too.

Lungworm is less common, and lives in the air passages of the lungs. Infected cats will wheeze and cough and appear very sickly.

Your vet will recommend a routine worming programme for your kitten to help keep him healthy. Treatments are in the form of granules, tablets, pastes, oral liquids, injections or spot-on applications, so there is something to suit every cat.

Kittens should be treated against roundworms at four to six weeks and then regularly every two to three weeks until they are four months old. After this worming they should be treated for roundworms and tapeworms every two to six months depending on how much they hunt and if they have fleas. Your vet will advise on the best wormer for you to use but always read and follow the instructions carefully.

Lice and ticks

If you have obtained your kitten from a reputable breeder he should not arrive with lice or ticks but as he ventures outside when he is older he may well pick these nasty creatures up. Lice are less common than fleas but are treated in the same way, with insecticides and grooming. As with fleas, treatments must be repeated to kill lice as they hatch out. They are visible to the naked eye and you will notice your kitten scratching to try to rid himself of the irritation.

Ticks are most common in the autumn and summer months and can transmit diseases, so get rid of them as soon as you can. A monthly treatment will help to reduce the risk of your cat picking these up. If you notice a tick on your cat, treat him with an appropriate insecticide (following the manufacturer's instructions carefully) and then wait until the tick is dead until you remove it with tweezers.

Top Cat Tip

Wear disposable rubber gloves or wash your hands thoroughly after treating your cat with insecticides.

Top Cat Tip

Do not 'layer' treatments by using more than one treatment at a time. This can increase the risk of your cat developing a toxic reaction to the products.

Ear mites

Ear mites are parasites with eight legs and are only just visible to the naked eye. Get into the habit of checking your kitten's ears on a weekly basis. They should normally be clean and pink and look slightly waxy in appearance. If you see any evidence of discharge or foul smell, this could indicate a bacterial or fungal infection. If you notice that your kitten is constantly shaking his head or scratching at his ears, or the presence of brown wax, this could indicate the presence of ear mites. Both of these conditions require veterinary treatment.

Diarrhoea

Your kitten may experience some diarrhoea during the first few days at home. This can be caused by stress but if it worsens or continues then it could be due to some other gastric problem such as an infection that requires medical treatment, so make an appointment for the kitten to be examined by a vet.

You can reduce the risk of gastric upset by offering your kitten the same brand of food that he ate at the breeders and feeding him small amounts little and often. Always introduce any dietary changes very slowly.

Ensure your kitten has free access to fresh, clean water to prevent him becoming dehydrated.

Signs of dehydration include: lethargy, panting, thirst, dull coat, tenting of the skin (i.e. there is reduced elasticity and if you pinch a fold of skin over the scruff of the neck it does not immediately fall back into position).

Untreated dehydration is very dangerous and can be fatal, so seek urgent veterinary advice if this is suspected.

Dental problems

Get your kitten used to having his gums handled and teeth cleaned early on to prevent the build-up of tartar and plaque. If you lift your kitten's lips away from his gums and press a finger over an upper tooth you should see a white imprint on the gum that quickly returns to a normal, healthy pink colour.

Look at the teeth to check for yellow or dark brown discolouration, which is an indication of tartar. Tartar needs to be removed by a vet, under anaesthesia, to help prevent painful gum disease.

Cat flu

Cat flu is a common problem, especially among unvaccinated cats. It is caused when cats are infected with either feline herpesvirus (formerly known as feline rhinotracheitis virus) and feline calicivirus. Occasionally cats are infected with both viruses. These viruses cause some cold-like symptoms such as a high temperature and sneezing but sometimes causes tongue ulcers. Thankfully most cats make a full recovery from this nasty illness, although it can take some weeks and can be fatal in very young kittens or older cats with a compromised immune system. The best way to prevent cat flu is by vaccinating against the two viruses responsible for its transmission.

Seasonal hazards

The changing seasons will affect your cat's behaviour and can produce different health problems. For example, in the summer your cat will naturally respond to hot weather by becoming less active during the day. He will probably be at his most active early in the morning and at dusk when the temperature starts to drop slightly. Older cats who become less active in the summer months but still consume the same amount of calories may start to put on extra weight.

Seasonal health and safety tips

- Unlike humans cats do not cool down by evaporation of sweat from their skin as they only sweat through the pads of their feet. Grooming helps cats to cool down, as the saliva they lick onto their coats evaporates and helps lower their body temperature slightly. Take care that your cat always has access to shaded areas, particularly if he enjoys sunbathing in a conservatory or on a hot windowsill.

- Water can evaporate very quickly in hot weather so refill water bowls more frequently.

- Longhair cats such as Persians may find the hot temperatures of summer more difficult to deal with than other breeds. Take steps to groom them more and keep rooms in the house as cool as possible.

- Remember that if you are travelling with your cat in the car, perhaps to take him to the vet, the temperature inside a car can quickly become unbearable. If a cat is in a carrier he is very vulnerable so never leave your car parked in sunshine.

- Cats walking through the long grass during late summer and early autumn often pick up ticks and mites so remain vigilant and treat as necessary.

- Your cat is vulnerable to sunburn on his ears and nose, particularly if he has white fur. Cats can also be vulnerable to developing skin cancer due to over-exposure to the sun. Protect white ears tips and noses with a quality non-toxic sun block developed especially for cats.

- Your cat will be enjoying the great outdoors more in the summer and may try climbing a few trees. Unfortunately some cats are better at climbing up trees than they are at getting back down again. If this happens do not panic, but do try to wait until evening before you attempt to rescue him as he may well come down when it is dark. In the UK it is advisable to call the RSPCA animal welfare charity rather than emergency services as they will not come out unless they are asked to do so by the RSPCA. If you think the cat is likely to fall, hold a duvet out under the tree to break his fall.

Did you know?

Cats find it more difficult to climb down trees because of the way their claws are designed. Claws make excellent grappling hooks when the cat is climbing up but because they point backwards are absolutely useless to him when he wants to come back down. Cats will not reverse down trees in case there is a predator waiting for them at the bottom, so instead they resort to slithering down in a rather inelegant fashion and then jumping the last few feet.

- Ensure you only use pet-friendly pesticides or weed killers and keep your cat indoors for several hours after you have used them.
- Ingestion of creosote can be fatal to cats. If you are painting fences or gateposts with creosote always ensure that your cat is safely shut indoors. Even ingesting a small amount by licking it off his paws can make him very ill. If you suspect your cat has creosote on his coat do not be tempted to use white spirits or turpentine to try to clean it off. Wrap him in a towel to prevent him from grooming himself and ask your vet for advice.
- Only use pet-friendly slug pellets that are harmless to cats and other wildlife.
- If your cat lives indoors all the time make sure you open the windows so that he can enjoy the feel of breathing in fresh air. If necessary have some wire mesh window screens fitted so that he remains safely inside.
- Vets report a dramatic increase in the number of cats they see in summer that have been injured because of a fall from a balcony. If you live in a high-rise apartment ensure that it is safe by fitting wire mesh around the sides and supervising his visits onto the balcony.
- Cats are always curious about buzzing insects and love to investigate what they are. If the insect happens to be a wasp or a bee the cat's nosiness often ends up with sting on the end

of their paws, nose or mouth area. Stings are painful but rarely dangerous although some cats may develop an allergic reaction, which will require veterinary treatment.

- In the winter older cats are more prone to the effects of cold. Always towel them off thoroughly if they come home wet and put an extra fleecy blanket on their bed to keep them warm.
- The holiday season brings its own hazards, particularly if you like to bring a real Christmas tree into your home. Fallen pine needles can easily become lodged into your cat's paws, so check them regularly.

figure 3 kittens find Christmas baubles totally irresistible ...

- Christmas trees can be very tempting to cats of all ages! It is the bright lights, shimmering tinsel and those tempting coloured baubles that look so attractive. Try to supervise your kitten when he is in the same room as the Christmas tree. If not, he may just decide to climb up it and bring the whole lot crashing down.
- Be especially careful when hanging strands of fairy lights. It is advisable to plug them into a circuit breaker in case your kitten decides to chew at the electric flex.
- After a summer barbeque dispose of any cooked meat and bones immediately. At Christmas, keep your cat out of the kitchen and do not allow him to eat poultry bones, which can easily splinter and become stuck in his mouth or throat resulting in internal injuries.

Did you know?

Bathing wasp stings in a dilute solution of vinegar in water will ease the discomfort. Bee stings will be neutralized by bathing with a weak dilution of bicarbonate of soda (baking soda).

Kittens and nutrition

In order for your kitten to live a long, healthy and happy life it is important that he is fed a nutritionally balanced diet. Because kittens grow so quickly (they increase their body weight by about 100 g/week in the first few weeks) and are so active they need food that can satisfy their requirements for energy, protein, fat, vitamins and minerals. Luckily, there are now specially developed kitten foods that have been formulated to cope with all your kitten's needs and these are readily available from supermarkets and other retail outlets.

What he needs

The ideal diet for humans is considered to be low fat, high fibre, but for cats it is the other way round. Cats need a diet with a high fat content to supply them with energy and lower fibre content to maintain their intestines.

Cats need proteins from amino acids for cell and tissue growth, as well as to help maintain and repair them. They also metabolize amino acids to give them energy. Cats require 20 amino acids and 11 of these are essential amino acids, which are not synthesized in the body. Meat, fish, eggs and milk are good sources of protein for cats but it is important to remember that cats are carnivores and will not cope well on a vegetarian diet. Cats are unable to produce taurine, an essential amino acid that is only available in meat. Deficiency in taurine produces visual disturbances and heart disease.

How much?

Non-pedigree kittens are often allowed to go to their new home at around eight weeks of age and because they are still so tiny will need five small meals a day. Pedigree kittens leave the breeder when they are older, probably at around 12 to 16 weeks of age and will often be down to four meals a day. It can be very useful if the breeder supplies you with a diet sheet for you to follow, along with other advice on how to care for him.

Kittens can sometimes develop allergies if their diets are changed suddenly, so always introduce changes very slowly, offering one new food at a time in small amounts. It is easier if your cat is willing to eat different foods, as if he is only keen on one particular brand he can develop into a fussy eater. You may also find yourself unable to cater for him if that brand becomes unavailable or the formula is changed.

You should feed your kitten first thing in the morning, at midday, mid-afternoon, at teatime and again in the evening. By the time he is six months old you can gradually reduce his feeds to morning and evening.

Top Cat Tip

Buy an easily recognizable spoon or fork to dish out your cat's food and keep this implement separate from your other crockery.

Wet or dry?

You can choose whether to feed wet or dry food or a combination of the two. Dried food, available in pouches, can be very convenient to use and has the advantage of not deteriorating quickly, so it can be left out all day and the kitten is able to return to it whenever he wants to. Canned wet food should be removed after half an hour, particularly in warm weather when flies and bacteria can quickly contaminate it.

If you have removed a can of wet food from the refrigerator, do not feed it to your kitten straight away but allow it to warm to room temperature first.

When it comes to how much to feed, do not make an educated guess. Follow the instructions on the labelling of the food carefully, to avoid under or over-feeding. It is quite easy to over-feed dried food, although it is relatively rare for kittens to become overweight as they are very active and burn off excess calories. However, it is easy to overload tiny stomachs so do not guess at the amount you are supposed to feed. Pet food companies spend a fortune researching exactly this, so take advantage of all their hard work!

Get your kitten into a regular routine, feeding him at the same times each day and putting him outside or onto his litter tray afterwards. Feed him in a quiet area of the house that is easy for you to clean.

Top Cat Tip

Always wash and rinse out his food and water bowls every day to help prevent gastric upset. It is more hygienic if you wash his bowls separately from your own crockery and keep a special brush just for this job.

Supplements

Commercially prepared complete kitten food has been formulated to contain all the vitamins and minerals your kitten needs so there should be no need to feed any extra supplements. Feeding non-essential supplements can upset the balance of the food and cause gastric problems so it is best to avoid unnecessary additives.

Treats

Your kitten will enjoy the occasional treat and they can be very useful, particularly when you are teaching him something new or trying to ensure that he comes when called. It is recommended that treats do not exceed more than 5 per cent of his total dietary intake. You can buy special cat treats from supermarkets or you may like to offer something fresh such as a tasty prawn or a few pieces of cooked chicken or fish.

Kitten milk

Unfortunately, although the cat that got the cream may have looked happy at the time, he probably did not later on when he experienced a nasty bout of diarrhoea! Kittens and cats are unable tolerate the lactose in cow's milk very well so if you do want to treat him to a drink of milk, buy one of the commercially prepared kitten milk formulas that are now readily available from supermarkets and pet discount stores.

Fresh water is vital to your kitten, so put a bowl of this down next to his feed bowl every day. This is particularly important if you are feeding one of the complete dried kitten foods that are available as he will be more thirsty.

Top Cat Tip
Put down several water bowls around the house, so that if your kitten gets locked into a room he always has access to a drink.

Top Cat Tip
Experiment to see if your cat prefers drinking filtered, distilled or bottled water.

03

all the fun
of the care

In this chapter you will learn:
- about house training
- games to play with your cat
- how to care for your cat.

Training

House training

Most kittens are naturally fastidious creatures and therefore very easy to house train. Unlike puppies most of them are already fully trained when they arrive in their new homes, making life much easier for owners. However, there must always be allowances for accidents, particularly if a kitten is not well or was locked in a room.

If your kitten soils in the house a lot, the first thing to do is to get him checked over by a vet to rule out any physical causes for this problem. Once he has received the all clear your vet may offer you advice or suggest referral to a pet behaviour counsellor who specializes in treating cats.

Sometimes inappropriate soiling with urine or faeces is a way for a cat to mark his territory. Indoor urine spraying is usually associated with a characteristic upright stance, but can be done when squatting as well.

figure 4 some cats are very fussy when it comes to using the facilities!

Changes to your kitten's routine or home environment can be stressful for him to deal with and may result in inappropriate soiling or territory marking.

Kittens that have had a poor example from their mothers or have been taken away from them too early may experience house-training problems. Sometimes reviewing the type of cat litter you use and the position of the litter tray can help to resolve the situation. Always place litter trays in a safe, private location and fill them with enough litter for the cat to be able to dig a hole in and subsequently rake over. Some cats prefer the privacy of a hooded tray to make them feel more secure and confident about using it.

They do not like being disturbed while on the litter tray, so choose an area that is not high traffic with other people and animals constantly going past. In addition, do not position the litter tray close to his food and water bowls, as this can discourage him from using it.

If your kitten does have an accident or misses the litter tray, do not get cross with him but clean the area quickly and thoroughly as this will discourage him from going back to the same place. Many household cleaning agents contain ammonia and/or chlorine, which are the constituents of urine and may confuse the cat. Instead, wash the area with a warm, biological detergent solution and, when it is dry, wipe over with surgical spirit (but always do a test patch on your carpet first).

Outdoor toilet

If you want your kitten to toilet outside, try mixing clean litter with small amounts of soil from the garden. Gradually increase the amount of soil but do not be tempted to use compost instead as this may encourage the kitten to use some of the plant pots in your house! Gradually move the litter tray closer to the door and then move it outside, putting your kitten on it every time he has eaten until he gets the idea of where you want him to go.

Back to basics

If a kitten has developed a long-standing habit of not using the litter tray it may be useful to restart his house training all over again by confining him to a large indoor crate or kennel for a few days. Place his bed, food and water bowls at one end and the litter tray at the other. Faced with limited choices of where he can go the kitten should be encouraged to start using the tray and can then gradually be reintroduced to using the tray outside of the pen.

Clicker training cats

Many people think it is not possible to train cats in the same way as dogs, but this is not true. Cats are extremely intelligent animals, highly motivated by food and with time and patience can be taught many tricks and commands. Clicker training is a relatively new method, internationally recognized by scientists who refer to it as operant conditioning.

There are many different types of clicker available, but essentially they are small, lightweight, hand-held plastic boxes, which when pressed down in the middle make a clicking noise. The training works by identifying a behaviour you want the cat to do, such as come to you, paying him with a high value treat such as a tasty piece of food or a favourite toy and then immediately clicking. The click becomes associated with the behaviour, which you then mark with a verbal command, such as 'here' or 'come'.

The key to successful clicker training is the accurate timing of the clicks, which should be done the second an animal performs something you want him to do. It may help to think of the clicker as a tiny camera, and when you press it at the right time you 'snap' and record the behaviour you want so that you can get the cat to repeat it again later. Press it too late and you are clicking something entirely different, such as the cat walking away from you.

Before you begin clicker training the cat get used to handling the clicker and test your accuracy with it. Try throwing a ball into the air and clicking before it hits the ground again.

Keep training sessions short, and schedule them for a time just before your cat is to be fed so he is a little hungry. Prepare some tiny high value treats of chicken, cheese or prawns and put them in a small pot. Throw one or two down for the cat so that he knows you have them. The next time, simultaneously click as you offer him a treat.

On target

You can try holding something out for the cat to touch, such as a pencil or a wooden spoon. As soon as the cat's nose touches the target, click and give him a reward. Do not do or say anything else to the cat, but repeat the exercise several times. He will soon realize what you want him to do and will start nudging the target to get you to click and give him a treat. You can mark the behaviour with a verbal command such as 'touch' or 'nudge'. With practice you can train him to walk around the room with you, following the target stick as he does so. You can also get him to jump over your arm or from one piece of furniture to another. In time you can train the cat to follow your hand rather than a target stick and you may be able to get him to reach up with one paw and give you a high five.

Top Cat Tip

Rubbing the end of the target stick with something tasty will encourage the cat to touch it. After the training session has ended put the target stick where the cat is unable to find it. If he touches it, hears no click and gets no treat he will soon become disinterested and may not co-operate the next time you bring the target stick out.

Free-style

It can also be fun to sit down with your cat in a free-style session and just watch him playing with his toys. You can click and mark behaviours that you like and want him to repeat, such as rolling over, playing football or retrieving a piece of rolled up paper for you. Simply throw the ball and give a verbal command such as 'fetch' then click and reward as soon as the cat returns to you with the ball in his mouth. Some cats really enjoy these free-style sessions and will start performing all kinds of acrobatic tricks in order to earn themselves a click and a treat.

Clicker training is a fascinating subject and entire books have been written about it. It is an excellent way of marking and positively reinforcing behaviours and encourages cats to think for themselves, giving them extra mental and physical stimulation and helping improve how they communicate with their owners. Some cats take to clicker training better than others but it can be a lot of fun so why not give it a try!

Social animals

If you have obtained your kitten from a reputable breeder he should already by quite well socialized and used to all kinds of different people, noises and situations. Continue this work at home to help build the bond of trust between you and help him become a confident adult cat. Here are some more ways you can continue his education:

- Invite as many different types of people as you can to handle your kitten and ask them to give him a treat. Include children, teenagers, the postman, older people and someone who is wearing a hat or glasses or carrying a stick.
- Let him watch as you put an umbrella up and down again.
- Play some loud music and, if you can, a CD of fireworks being set off.
- Accustom him to going in and out of his carrier (see page 49).
- Play different kinds of games with him, such as retrieving, chasing, hunting, etc.
- Put him in a secure pet carrier and take him out in the car for short journeys.
- Introduce him to your neighbour's dogs (if they're friendly) or other pets such as rabbits.
- Encourage children to practise playing their musical instruments when the kitten is in the room.
- Handle the kitten's paws, gums and ticklish areas so that he accepts this without a problem.
- Ask different people to groom, feed and play with the kitten to encourage him to bond with other family members.
- Take him in the garden and introduce him to outdoor life.
- Gently flap the laundry out towards him, as you hang it out on the line to dry.
- Ring door bells and ask people to walk in and out of the room, past the kitten.
- Get him used to the television and radio playing and the telephone ringing.

Playing games with your cat

You and the rest of your family will have a lot of fun playing with your kitten and his antics will cause much hilarity. This is a great opportunity for you to use your imagination, be inventive and find your inner kitten!

Play is not just a fun activity, though. It helps kittens to develop their social interaction skills and it is important that they have the opportunity to learn how to manipulate different types of toys and throw them in the air. It will increase his eye/paw co-ordination skills and help him to burn off energy. Schedule play sessions before he has eaten but respect the fact that he needs to sleep a lot when he is little, so do not wake him just because the time suits you.

Cats are naturally more predatory at dawn and dusk, so will probably be more interested in playing at these times. It is better to have two or three playtime sessions of 10 to 15 minutes rather than one long session that only finishes when the cat becomes tired, bored and disinterested.

Invest in a selection of different toys to help him exercise his natural prey-chasing and hunting tendencies. It is a good idea to keep your kitten's toys in a special toy box or basket and rotate the ones that are available to him all the time so that he does not get bored with them.

Have a variety of toys, such as interactive or puzzle ones that he has to move around to get treats out of, fishing-rod-style toys that he has to stand up and try to catch, and hunting games where you drag something along the ground for him to try to capture, as well as retrieval games where you throw something for him to fetch. Cats also enjoy playing with squeaky toys, but avoid anything that is too loud or that may frighten him.

Top Cat Tip

Do not allow your kitten to bite or scratch you when he is playing. If this happens simply say no, stop interacting with him and end the session so that he associates biting with loss of attention from you. What can seem like fun, cute behaviour in a kitten will not be so endearing when he is a large, adult cat so consistently discourage unwanted, boisterous behaviour from the start.

King of the castle

Although you can purchase expensive cat activity centres, it is easy to entertain your cat by making him a castle from cardboard boxes. Simply find a sturdy box or two, glue them together and then cut round holes out for him to climb in and out of. Throw some toys or treats through the holes and watch as curiosity gets the better of him and he disappears inside to investigate!

Treasure hunt

Try hiding some tasty treats around the room for your cat to find. Lay a trail around the house and gradually make it more challenging for him to reach and retrieve the titbits he is after.

Obstacle race

Use boxes, ladders, hoops and tubes to construct a little obstacle course for your kitten to go round. Children will enjoy helping you do this. Encourage your kitten with treats so that he races through the course to see what is at the other end!

Bubble trouble

Buy some children's bubble mixture and have fun blowing them for your kitten to chase. Believe it or not you can now even buy a special bubble mixture that has been developed just for cats, and the bubbles smell of catnip!

figure 5 OK, where do bubbles go when they pop?

Glitter balls

Cats enjoy chasing those little balls that bounce high and light up or make a noise to catch their attention. However, they will also have a lot of fun with a plain ping-pong ball or a ball made of scrunched-up newspaper. Avoid using silver foil or clingfilm as these can be dangerous if swallowed.

Although there are lots of fishing-rod-style toys available to buy, you can have a lot of fun and save yourself some money by making them. Simply find a long twig from the garden, tie some string or elastic around it and thread cotton reels, a ping-pong ball or some feathers on the bottom. Trail the string along the ground and watch as your cute little kitten turns into the Lion King as he stalks and kills his prey! This game will be more realistic to him as the 'prey' appears to be creeping along the ground and will not be associated with something you are holding in your hand. The hunting instinct is not always stimulated by hunger, but by movement or noise, so he will not mind that he cannot eat it once he has captured and killed it!

Without this kind of play to satisfy his natural hunting instinct your kitten could well become frustrated and start pouncing on your feet or other pets as they walk past.

Do not forget that no matter how many toys you provide for your kitten, he will always add to the collection by finding his own. Your laundry basket or dressing table with its array of blusher brushes, bottle tops and other interesting items will be a source of rich pickings! Tidy away anything you do not want him to get hold of or that may be dangerous to him if swallowed.

Top Cat Tip

If your cat loses interest in one of his toys take it away from him for a few days and rejuvenate it with a spray of catnip.

Top Cat Tip

Do not encourage your cat to pounce on your toes or fingers, either by deliberately moving them under the bed covers or running them along the side of the sofa. He will enjoy doing this so much he will probably decide to ambush your feet when you are walking through the house. Not too much of a problem when he is a kitten, but not so much fun when he is a fully grown adult cat!

Did you know?

If your cat shows prowess at negotiating an obstacle course he may well be a promising participant in a Cat Agility competition. This new sport is becoming popular in the USA and is designed to show off the grace, athleticism and beauty of cats in motion, as well as expand the human–feline bond. Watch out for the sport making its way over to Europe!

Grooming

How much grooming your kitten requires each week will depend on his coat type. If he is a shorthaired kitten you need only give him a brush and comb once or twice a week, whereas semi-longhaired cats need to be groomed two or three times a week and longhaired cats such as Persians need to be groomed every day, and sometimes even twice a day if they are allowed outside.

Just because you have a shorthair kitten does not mean you cannot groom him every day if you want to and there is no doubt that if done gently and calmly from an early age, it will help to improve your relationship.

How to groom your cat

- Before you start, gather together all your grooming equipment. See Chapter 02, page 32 for details of what your kit should include. It is a good idea to keep all the kit together in a bag or box so that you are not searching around each time trying to locate different brushes and combs.
- In addition to the grooming kit, get a clean bowl of tepid water ready, together with some cotton wool balls.
- Choose a time to groom when you and the cat are feeling relaxed. Do not groom him when he is over-tired or feeling hungry, but perhaps in the evening when you are sitting together watching the television or even outside in the garden on a sunny afternoon.
- Start the session by just stroking him and using your voice to calm and relax him. It is essential that he learns to enjoy being groomed and does not become tense or worried by the experience, otherwise he will start hiding every time he sees the grooming box come out! If you have bought a longhair kitten pedigree hopefully the breeder will already have introduced him to being groomed, so you should not experience too many problems.

- Check each one of his paws, to make sure he has no cuts on his pads or pieces of gravel or cat litter stuck between them. Gently dislodge any debris that has gathered there.

- As you stroke the cat, check inside his ears to ensure there are no signs of ear mites (see Chapter 02, page 53).

- Using separate cotton wool balls each time, wipe the kitten's eyes, going from the inside of the eye to the outside. Alternatively you can buy special disposable eye wipes designed to help clean this delicate area. Seek veterinary advice if there are signs of infection or discharge.

- Now select a brush that will help to massage the skin and remove any loose dead hair from the coat. You will need something like a soft bristle brush, a rubber brush or a slicker brush for this job.

- Use a metal flea comb all over the coat, always following the direction of the fur. You are looking for those telltale black spots in the dead hair you remove.

- Now use a wide-tooth metal comb to gently untangle the fur around his armpits, chest and tummy. These are sensitive and ticklish areas so take your time, giving the kitten a break if necessary before returning to finish the job. Continue to talk to him gently and calmly to help reassure him. Offer him a tasty treat to reward him for being patient.

- Check his back end to ensure it is clean, particularly if he has experienced any gastric problems. If necessary wash this area in a solution of warm water and cat shampoo. Use round-ended scissors to snip away any of the coat that is badly matted. You can also wipe the area with a special deodorizing wipe but only use products that have been developed for use on cats in this delicate area.

- Now put on a disposable rubber glove and gently stroke your kitten's gums, encouraging him to allow you to examine his teeth. Check that there are no signs of broken or missing teeth. Just do this for a few seconds at first and as time goes on increase the time until you are able to use a special cat toothbrush and toothpaste to keep his teeth and gums healthy and sweet smelling.

- End the grooming session either by smoothing his coat with your hands, a chamois leather or a grooming mitt. Some people like to put a drop or two of baby oil on the cloth to add a little extra sheen. You can also buy grooming wipes saturated in a natural flea repellent, such as citronella, eucalyptus and citric oils, which may help to keep those annoying creatures at bay.

Top Cat Tip

Cats with longhair coats can develop knots and tangles very easily, especially at the inside tops of their legs. It may be necessary to cut into these tangles to help comb them out. Ask someone to hold the cat to keep him still and only use round-ended grooming scissors to do this job. Make a single cut into the knot towards the skin and then use your fingers to gently tease out the tangles.

Bathing a cat

For most domestic cats it is not necessary to bathe them unless they get particularly dirty. Excessive bathing can remove essential oils from the coat and so it is important to groom thoroughly afterwards to encourage the secretion of sebaceous oils that will keep the coat waterproof and glossy. Longhair cats and show cats will require bathing once a month or on the day before a show to help keep their coats tangle-free and in top-class condition.

- Always comb the cat thoroughly before you bathe him. If you bathe him before you try to comb out the tangles you will find that they have dried and 'set' and will be much more difficult to remove.

- Get everything you need ready before you start and enlist the help of a friend if you think you will not be able to manage on your own. There is nothing more frustrating than a wet, sudsy cat diving for cover under the sofa and refusing to come out again!

- You can bathe your cat in the kitchen sink if you want to, but place a towel or rubber mat in the bottom so that he can grip this with his claws. It will make him feel more stable and secure and you will be able to hold him better.

- A baby's bath is also ideal for bathing a cat in and these can be obtained second hand very easily. Another alternative is to use a deep plastic storage crate.

- Fill the bath with water that is not too hot or cold and then put the cat in. Wet the coat with a sponge or by pouring a jug of water onto the coat. Avoid getting any water into the cat's eyes or ears.

- Always use a good quality cat shampoo and never be tempted to use one of your own fragrant-smelling hair products. Cats are very sensitive animals and unable to break down many chemical components found in everyday products. Shampoos that contain products such as tea tree oil that have not been diluted sufficiently may be very toxic to cats when they lick their coats afterwards.

- Thoroughly massage the shampoo into the cat's coat, avoiding the eyes and ears.
- Rinse the coat thoroughly and if necessary use a second application of shampoo. A hose attachment on the taps is ideal for rinsing the coat with clean water.
- When you have finished, lift the cat out and wrap him in a thick towel. It is important to keep the cat warm until he is completely dry. Towel off any excess water and if the cat will allow you, use a hair drier to dry him more quickly. Put the drier on the lowest temperature setting and move it along the cat's body in the direction of the fur.
- Finally, use a slicker brush to work through the coat, removing any dead hairs and fluffing the coat up. Start at the cat's head and work along the body towards the tail but be particularly careful around the cat's head.

Massage

You can also take the opportunity to pamper your cat with a relaxing massage. This is particularly beneficial for older cats, as their joints tend to get stiffer and they lose muscle tone and flexibility. Simply use the tips or pads of your first two fingers to apply gentle pressure and work your way all the way down each of his legs until you reach his paws. Take the paws in your hands and gently pull them through your fingers. You will be able to tell by your cat's body language whether or not he is enjoying this; some cats purr like mad and others find it ticklish or uncomfortable, in which case it is best to move to another part of the body.

Top Cat Tip

You can buy massage brushes, which help to groom the cat as well as giving them a relaxing therapy session. They tend to have chunky rubber finger bristles and are available from most good pet stores or retail outlets.

Caring for claws

If you have provided your cat or kitten with a scratch post or he has access to outdoors and some tree trunks or gate posts, he should be able to keep his claws filed and in good condition. Claws are made from keratin (the same material as hair) and are used to help the cat maintain his balance when he walks on his toes. Cats will naturally shed the outer skin of their claws rather than wear them down and most people who clip claws are doing so unnecessarily and also encouraging the cat to scratch more and sharpen them up again.

Older cats or indoor cats may need some help to keep their claws at a reasonable length so that they do not start growing into their pads or make walking difficult. If you do decide to clip your cat's claws only use clippers that have been specifically designed for this purpose.

Hold the cat confidently and firmly and press the pad of his paw so that the nails are pushed out (see Plate 13). Only clip across the very top of the claw, and avoid the pinkish quick which contains nerves and will bleed if cut. If you make a mistake and cut into the quick, press it with a cotton wool ball or tissue paper pad until the bleeding stops.

Your vet or a practice nurse will happily clip your cat's claws for you if you are not confident or want to be given a practical demonstration. See Chapter 05 for a step-by-step guide on how to clip your cat's claws.

> **Top Cat Tip**
>
> If you intend to show your cat the judges will expect you to clip his claws as part of his preparation for the competition.

Dental care

Bad breath (halitosis) is one of the most common reasons that a cat is taken to the vet although sadly many owners never bother to look inside their cat's mouth. Gingivitis (inflammation of the gums) and dental disease caused by an accumulation of tartar (hard deposits made from the minerals in food and saliva), plaque from undigested food and bacteria are the most common problems.

In the early stages you may notice some brown staining of the cat's teeth and bad breath but as the deposits continue to accumulate they start to impinge on the gums, causing them to become red, inflamed and painful.

Gingivitis causes the gums to recede, which can expose the crown of the teeth normally buried inside the gum. Bacteria can build up in these areas and cause infection, sometimes to such an extent that the tooth falls out.

It is not known why some cats develop dental problems more than others although there is no doubt that diet and genetics play a large part. Cats with severe gingivitis can find eating very painful and difficult and some can hardly eat at all, causing weight loss and other health problems.

Good dental hygiene is therefore very important to keep your cat healthy. Although some people argue that cats in the wild survive quite happily without having their teeth cleaned, this is not quite true, as wild cats do not enjoy the longevity of domestic pets. Because they die so much younger dental problems are not common.

Vets have noted that cats fed on wet, soft food have a significantly increased risk of dental problems than those fed on dry food. It is thought that the abrasive texture of cat biscuits helps to stop the build-up of tartar and plaque.

By introducing your kitten to tooth cleaning from a young age, you will be giving him the very best start to help keep his teeth and gums healthy. However, do not become depressed or feel frustrated if your cat still develops a build-up of tartar that requires descaling under a light anaesthetic. No matter how hard you try, it is sometimes impossible to prevent a cat developing some form of dental problems. Thankfully, modern anaesthetics are much safer now and recovery from them is much quicker.

Top Cat Tip

Never be tempted to use human toothpaste on your cat as this will froth up and he will find the taste extremely unpleasant, making it unlikely that he will co-operate in the future.

Neutering

Unfortunately cat charities and shelters are always full of unwanted kittens. This could so easily be avoided if owners will only do the responsible thing and get their cats neutered. The benefits of neutering are huge both to the individual cat and future generations.

> **Did you know?**
> The term for neutering a male cat is castration, while a female cat is referred to as being spayed.

Benefits

A female cat that has not been spayed and does not have a litter of kittens may go on to develop phantom pregnancies and/or womb infections. Left unspayed the cat will come into season every few weeks and experience bleeding, agitation and frustration, which will often manifest itself by her calling out noisily with a low-pitched yowl. Your little puss will also be at greater risk of other serious health problems in later life, such as mammary (breast) cancer.

An entire (uncastrated) male cat will roam in search of a mate, and can develop antisocial behaviour such as aggression or evidence of sexual frustration including mounting other pets and even people! Because of the tendency to roam he will be at increased risk of injury through fighting, car accidents and serious health problems such as prostate cancer. Entire males have a strong 'tomcat' smell, which is unpleasant and very noticeable in the owner's house.

Neutering was always traditionally carried out when a cat reached sexual maturity at the age of six months but these days it is often done much earlier. Because of improved safety and efficacy in anaesthetics and surgical techniques, neutering is sometimes carried out as early as eight to 12 weeks and no adverse side effects have been reported as a result of this. Your vet will be able to advise when he thinks it is appropriate for your cat to be neutered. There is no upper age limit to having your cat neutered, provided he is healthy and able to cope with the anaesthetic.

During surgery, under anaesthetic the testes of a male cat are removed through a single cut into the scrotum. It is a straightforward procedure and does not usually require any stitching.

For female cats a single cut into the belly is applied and the ovaries and uterus are removed. It is a more complicated procedure than for a male cat and stitches are usually required, but your vet will do this so regularly that it is a routine procedure for him to carry out.

Both male and female cats are usually allowed home the same day, after the effects of the anaesthetic have worn off. Female cats return to the surgery within seven to ten days to have their stitches removed and to be examined to make sure all is well.

Myths

It is a myth to think that neutering or spaying will somehow dramatically alter your cat's character although he or she will be more relaxed and less frustrated. Monitoring and adjusting your cat's diet and exercise levels will ensure that he does not put on too much weight after neutering. It is also a myth that female cats should be allowed to have at least one litter of kittens. Research has shown no health or psychological benefits to this.

Microchipping

One of the very best things you can do for your cat is to get him microchipped as soon as you possibly can. It is not a particularly expensive procedure, causes only a moment of minor discomfort to the cat and gives you, the owner, a lifetime of security. Even indoor cats can escape if a visitor leaves the door or window open, so it is worth getting all cats microchipped.

The procedure can be carried out by your vet, a practice nurse or by an authorized organization such as a charity or rescue centre. Unlike a collar, a microchip cannot be removed, altered or easily lost so it is much more difficult for cases of mistaken identity to occur if a cat is lost or stolen.

When you arrive for your appointment, your vet will simply inject a microchip that is approximately the size of a grain of rice under the skin between your cat's shoulder blades. Details of the microchip and the owner's address and contact details will then be registered with the database of the company your vet or charity uses. It is important to remember to notify the database holders of any changes to your personal details such as moving to a new address, so that they are able to contact you if the cat goes missing and is later found and scanned.

When the microchip has been injected your vet will use a special scanner to transmit a radio signal through the skin to read the chip. Once the microchip number has been detected it is then relayed to the scanner.

Ask your vet to check the microchip every time you visit to ensure that it is still in place. Early microchips occasionally migrated around the body and became 'lost' but many are now made with an anti-migrating cap or coating to help prevent this.

There have been hundreds of heart-warming stories of lost cats being reunited with their owners because a microchip scanner has been used to identify them successfully. It really is a worthwhile expense and may even result in a slight discount on your insurance policy.

Top Cat Tip

If you intend to travel abroad with your cat and want to bring him back home to the UK it is a legal requirement that you have him microchipped. Always ensure that the microchip being used meets the standards recognized by the International Standards Organization (ISO). Most vets in Europe will use ISO recognized chips that can be read by compatible scanners.

Top Cat Tip

The UK is the only country in Europe where people other than vets are allowed to microchip pets (although this also occurs in the USA). If you allow someone other than a vet to microchip your cat, ask them what training they have had and whether they have a proficiency certificate issued by the microchip distributor company.

What to do if your cat goes missing

It can be a very frightening experience for an owner to discover that their cat or kitten has gone missing. It is important to try not to panic though, as most of the time he will simply be hiding from you or enjoying a lovely sleep somewhere in your house or garden! While your blood pressure goes through the ceiling he is probably snoozing happily in a very comfy hidey-hole that you know nothing about.

Begin by arming yourself with a box of biscuits that you can rattle noisily, and go all round the house shouting his name. Stop periodically to listen in silence and notice if you can hear a faint miaow. If you cannot find him on the first search move out into the garden and repeat the entire exercise several times.

Once you have decided that the cat is definitely missing there are several things you can do:

- Ask family, friends and neighbours to help you by searching their houses, outbuildings and gardens.
- Telephone your vet and other local veterinary surgeries to see if a cat that matches your cat's description has been brought in following an accident.
- Telephone local animal shelters to report your cat missing and see if he has been found. Leave contact details so they can telephone you if he is discovered later and brought in.
- Use a recent photograph of the cat to make a flier containing details of when and where the cat was last seen. Photocopy and distribute these through letterboxes and post on trees throughout your neighbourhood.
- Draft an advertisement, preferably with a photograph, for the local paper. Consider offering a reward for your cat's return.
- Telephone national cat charities. Your cat may have clambered into a tradesman's van, fallen asleep and woken up miles away, so it is worth registering his details with as many organizations as you can.
- Call the database holder of the microchip company your cat is registered with to inform them your cat is missing.
- Widen your search but also return to areas you have already tried. Try searching at different times of day as a lost cat can take some weeks to establish himself and make himself noticed by people who live there. It may be that he has attached himself to someone who works shifts, so search at different times of the day and night to increase the chances of finding him.

If you do not find your cat after several weeks or months, it can be very distressing and you will undergo a grieving process not dissimilar to losing a cat through death. See Chapter 05 for tips and ideas on how to help you recover from your grief.

04

owning an adult cat

In this chapter you will learn:
- about health and nutrition
- about behaviour problems
- ten ways to keep your cat happy.

Taking on an adult cat

For various reasons you may have decided to give a home to an adult cat rather than a kitten. There is no doubt that, entertaining as they are, kittens have a lot of energy and can be hard work. Many people do not have the time or patience to train a livewire kitten and prefer the company of a more mature, settled puss.

If you know the cat's history, perhaps because he belonged to a neighbour who has gone into a nursing home where animals are not allowed or his owner has died, it may be relatively simple to adopt the cat and give him a happy second home. However, if you are taking on a rescue cat with an uncertain background you must be prepared to face more challenges as you get to know the cat, his personality and behaviour traits.

Another reason some people prefer to take on an adult cat is to replace a cat that has died, or because they are determined to give a needy cat a second chance in life. Owners who live in high-rise apartments with no garden areas may want an adult indoor cat that is already known to be quite happy to live in confined conditions.

Whatever the reason, people who want to take on an adult cat are always very welcome at animal shelters. Some older cats have been residents there for months and occasionally years, as cute kittens are the more popular choice. Cats with little chance of adoption include those who are old, disabled or have a pre-existing medical condition such as diabetes. None of these reasons preclude the cats from making wonderful pets and some rescue organizations will offer ongoing support and even contribute to the cost of veterinary care in order to get these cats rehomed.

The most common reasons a cat is in a shelter include:

- They were picked up as strays
- They have been abandoned
- Health problems
- The owner has developed allergies
- Divorce
- The owner has a new job and cannot care for the cat
- The owners emigrating
- Elderly owners going into a residential home
- Bereavement
- Behaviour problems.

plate 9 Known as the 'lazy man's Persian', who can resist an Exotic Shorthair?

plate 10 A cousin of the Siamese, the Oriental will certainly keep you entertained!

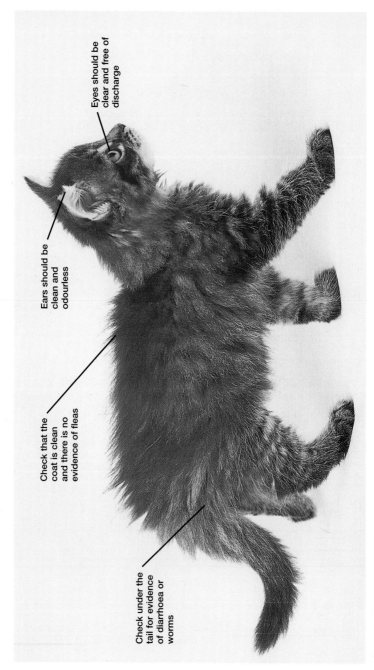

Eyes should be clear and free of discharge

Ears should be clean and odourless

Check that the coat is clean and there is no evidence of fleas

Check under the tail for evidence of diarrhoea or worms

plate 11 Kitten health check.

plate 12 Shade, foliage and sunshine help to make this lovely cat run a perfect retreat.

plate 13 Always use clippers that are designed specifically for cat's claws.

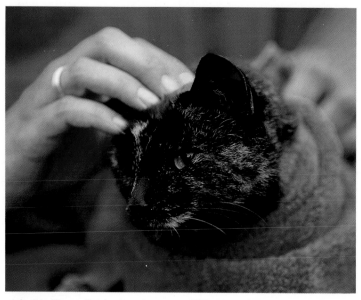

plate 14 The gentle, circular movements of T-Touch can help relax even the most defensive of cats.

plate 1   The sweet-natured, home-loving Ragoll.

plate 2   You need time and commitment to keep Persians looking this glamorous.

plate 3 The extrovert Siamese can demand lots of attention.

plate 4 The placid British Shorthair is a family favourite.

plate 5 The Bengal combines wild cat glamour with home-loving puss.

plate 6 The elegant Burmese is full of personality and grace.

plate 7 The majestic Birman is renowned for its personality and tolerance.

plate 8 The Maine Coon is a powerful-looking but characterful puss.

Once people have decided they would like to take on an adult cat, they are often surprised and frustrated that they cannot just walk into a shelter, choose a cat and go home with him. The fact is that rescue centres are very keen to get the right home for individual cats as they do not want the cat returned to them in a few weeks because the home is unsuitable. Be patient and co-operative as you may be expected to fill in a questionnaire, have an interview, accept a home visit and make a donation towards the expenses incurred by the centre. You may also be asked to sign an undertaking that you will ensure the cat is regularly wormed and vaccinated, etc.

Top Cat Tip

Ensure your cat has been microchipped before you take him home, in case he escapes and gets lost.

When it comes to preparing your home, collecting the cat and helping him to settle into his new home there are no differences to those of caring for a kitten. However, an adult cat, particularly one from a shelter, may take some weeks to gain confidence in his new owners so give him plenty of time and do not be disappointed if he does not appear to bond with you overnight. Give the cat as much time as he needs and do not try to pick him up and cuddle him if he is not ready for this. Behaviourists have found that a stronger bond is developed if the cat initiates contact with the owner, rather than the other way round, so sit quietly and wait for the cat to come to you.

Do not worry if your cat disappears behind the sofa and refuses to come out. He will be feeling very nervous, so just sit quietly, say his name and offer him a tasty treat to tempt him. Do not, under any circumstances, decide to haul him out before he is ready as he will find this extremely traumatic.

Some cats are so stressed by the experience of moving home that they completely lose their appetite for a few days. This is understandable but if you offer him the same food as he had at the rescue centre you will avoid the risk of tummy upsets. You can gradually introduce some new foods to tempt him with, such as a little poached fish or chicken.

> **Top Cat Tip**
>
> When you first take the cat home, make an effort to be particularly calm and reassuring. Help him to settle in by keeping your movements slow and steady, so that your cat is not startled or threatened in any way.

It is advisable to keep your new cat indoors until he has settled down and is completely confident in his new home and with everyone in the family.

Adult pedigree cats

Even if you have decided you would prefer an adult cat, there is no reason why you cannot have a pedigree of your choice. If you have your heart set on a particular breed, contact the breed society affiliated to it and ask to be put in touch with the welfare officer. Unfortunately people who own pedigrees are not exempt from life's traumas such as marriage breakdown, allergies and all the other reasons that cats are offered for rehoming. Sadly, they are also offered for rehoming because owners did not do their homework beforehand and then found they did not have the time, resources or ability to care for a high-maintenance breed. Breed clubs are always very concerned for the welfare of cats and usually have a list of cats they are trying to find new homes for. Have a chat with the welfare officer and ask for your name to be added to the list should a cat become available. Once again you may be asked to accept a home visit and be interviewed, but this is so that the cat is not made any more insecure than he already is by being put up for adoption again.

Feeding an adult cat

By the time a cat is six months old he can be fed just twice a day, which is usually first thing in the morning and early evening.

Depending on how active the cat is, most adult cats have a daily energy requirement of between 60 and 90 Kcal/kg body weight, but it is recommended that least a quarter of their diet should be in protein form. Typically, canned food provides around 70 Kcal/100 g.

Indoor cats often lead a less active lifestyle than cats that are allowed to go outside, and so their energy requirements are less – probably around 50 Kcals/kg/day. Pet food manufacturers are beginning to recognize this lifestyle and are now developing specially formulated diets for indoor cats. These indoor cat food formulas also take into account constant coat moulting, lower activity levels leading to slower digestion and a tendency to pile on extra weight.

It is possible to only feed your cat a home-cooked diet but unless you are very knowledgeable about the science of feline nutrition you could be causing him problems. For example, undercooking food can result in food poisoning and cooking food for too long can destroy some of the enzymes your cat needs and make the food indigestible.

Do not forget that if you feed your cat treats, these should be counted as part of his daily calorie intake!

Ideal weight

The normal weight of an adult cat will vary considerably depending on age, breed and lifestyle but should probably be around 4 kg for a small cat and around 5.5 kg for a larger type. However, it is worth remembering that some pedigree breeds can be very heavy, for example a male Norwegian Forest cat can weigh 6–10 kg, whereas a female will weigh half as much.

Obesity

Dealing with obesity

Your cat will be weighed when you take him for his annual check-up and your vet or the practice nurse will inform you if he is showing signs of middle-age spread. Carrying excessive weight puts a lot of strain on important vital organs such as the heart and if left unchecked will cause him a lot of health problems and shorten his life span.

figure 6 older cats have a tendency to pile on the pounds

Obesity problems include:

- Joint disease
- Heart problems
- Difficulty breathing
- Urinary tract disease
- Risk of diabetes.

If your cat has put on quite a lot of weight you will probably see signs of this with the naked eye. He may have accumulated fat cross his back, the ribs and underneath the belly. Some cats are so fat that their belly almost drags on the ground as they walk, which is extremely uncomfortable.

Preventing obesity

Keep your eye on your cat's weight between his surgery visits. It is easy to weigh a cat; if he is very obliging he may just sit quite happily on your bathroom scales but if not you can simply weigh his carrier and then put the cat inside, deducting his weight from the total.

It is not necessary to become so obsessed with your cat's weight that you are putting him on the scales every week, but get into the habit of weighing him every month or two and do not forget to write the figures down in a notebook or diary so you can monitor the situation and take action if required.

> ### Did you know?
> Any cat that is 15 per cent over his ideal weight is considered to be obese and, unbelievably, it is thought that almost half of the UK's cats fall into this category.

If your cat has put on too much weight you need to reduce his calorie intake and increase his activity levels. He will only lose weight if he is burning more calories than he is eating. Following pet food manufacturers' guidelines will help but cats vary enormously in how much food they need in order to maintain their weight at a reasonable level that you may have to experiment slightly. Your vet will be able to advise if you have any concerns about how much your cat should be eating and many clinics run pet obesity clinics designed specifically to help owners cope with overweight animals.

It's very important that you do not put your cat on a strict diet overnight and that you make any changes very gradually. As with human weight loss, a small, steady loss is considered to be better than a drastic loss and the cat is less likely to regain the weight. Learn how to resist if your cat begs to share some of your food. If he persists in miaowing, rubbing around your legs or resorting to standing on his back legs and trying to steal the food off your plate then it is probably worth putting him outside or in another room until your meal is finished.

> ### Top Cat Tip
> It is easy to overfeed dry foods. Although they are convenient to feed and good for the cat's teeth and gums they can alter the cat's natural weight-control mechanism, and result in obesity.

If yours is an indoor cat, you must increase his level of activity during play sessions. Try to involve him in some climbing and chasing games to help him shed the extra pounds but be careful if he is an older cat with joint problems. Aim for three ten-minute play sessions per day.

Top Cat Tip

If yours is an outdoor cat and is putting on weight, have a chat with some of your neighbours to find out whether he is paying them a visit during the day to try and get a few extra snacks! Cats can be quite convincing when it comes to asking for food and assuring people they have not been fed for days ...

Top Cat Tip

Nutritionists recommend that owners use a smaller bowl when feeding their cat. This will help to relieve the anxiety and guilt that you are somehow depriving him of a proper serving of food.

Did you know?

According to the *Guinness Book of Records* the heaviest domestic cat was a neutered male tabby named Himmy, from Queensland, Australia. When poor Himmy died of respiratory failure on 12 March 1986 at the age of 10 years, 4 months, he weighed 21.5 kg (neck 38 cm, waist 84 cm, length 96.5 cm). Life must have been very difficult for this fat feline.

A hunting we will go ...

As your cat grows, so may his interest and proficiency in hunting. Although most owners do not appreciate the gift of a dead bird being brought into the house or left on the doorstep, your cat will not understand your displeasure. It is hard to estimate the impact of cats on the birds and wildlife of the UK but one research study claims that as many as 275 million are despatched each year although birds comprise only about 20 per cent, the rest being small mammals such as mice and voles. A USA study claims that as many as 1.6 billion birds are killed annually. Despite these seemingly large numbers it is not thought that cats are having a direct impact on the bird population; many of the birds caught would have died anyway from natural causes.

Hunting is very much a part of your cat's natural instinct, although how much they hunt varies enormously and depends on the cat's age, personality and lifestyle. Although you cannot easily prevent your cat doing something that nature evolved him to do, there are a few things you can do to protect the birds and wildlife in your neighbourhood.

Protecting wildlife

- Keeping your cat indoors at dawn and dusk when birds are more likely to be feeding is a good start. This is particularly important during the months of March to May when they are breeding and also during December and January when food supplies are short.

- You should also try putting a collar with one or two bells on when he goes outside, to help alert birds that he is on the prowl. One survey reports that a collar with a bell could help reduce bird predation by up to one-third. Although there are also collars available that emit a sonic sound, it is not yet known how effective these are.

- There is no reason why cat owners cannot feed birds in their gardens as long as care is taken in the positioning of feeders. Avoid positioning a bird table or feeding station close to any low-lying shrubs or bushes, as these can provide excellent hiding places or cover for your cat as he prepares to pounce. Planting something like a prickly holly underneath a bird table can help deter cats.

Top Cat Tip

There is a theory that birds may be able to see the colour red better than other colours, and so putting a red collar on your cat may help protect them.

Top Cat Tip

Do not shout at your cat if he brings a mouse or birds into the house. He will not understand your anger. If you can rescue the bird, it will undoubtedly be in a state of shock and may die of this rather than any physical injuries. Put the bird into a dark, quiet box with air holes for half an hour or so and then remove the lid to see if the bird has recovered enough to fly away.

How your adult cat will behave

Some cats manage to retain kitten-like behaviour throughout their lives. In particular, Oriental breeds such as Siamese are renowned for remaining lively and curious creatures that demand lots of attention. Other breeds such as the Persian tend to become much more placid and are prepared to settle down and enjoy life at a far slower pace. While longhairs still enjoy lots of human contact and company they are not as demanding and have sunny dispositions that make them low maintenance in terms of their emotional needs.

As your cat matures he will develop sexual behaviour traits such as coming into season (for a female) and seeking to find a mate. By the time your cat is six months old he should be neutered (see Chapter 03 for further details on this procedure) or you may find he strays if left outdoors. Uncastrated males will fight and are at risk of injury from road accidents and disease. Your sweet little female cat will take to howling like a banshee as she lets you know in no uncertain terms how desperate she is to find a mate. She will also frantically try to escape from your home, scratching at doors and trying to get through windows. It is much kinder to get a cat neutered by the time he is six months old.

Depending on your cat's personality, breed, and lifestyle his activity levels may drop as he becomes older. This may not coincide with a decrease in his calorie intake and so adult cats are very vulnerable to middle-age spread. See above for more details on how to deal with obesity and help your cat lose any unwanted extra pounds.

If you have had your cat since he was a kitten he will have well and truly worked his way into your life and your heart by now. Most cats are very adept at training their owners and unless you are very careful, you could find that your cat is running your life as you prepare his meals, cancel dates, rush home to spend some quality time with him and even find yourself perched on the edge of the bed at night as he takes the lion's share of the covers. While it is lovely to enjoy a happy relationship with your cat, try to ensure that it remains balanced and that those ground rules you worked so hard to establish when he was a kitten are still being adhered to.

Cats are funny creatures and locations they enjoyed for several weeks or months as a kitten may suddenly, for no apparent reason, be abandoned in favour of a new 'favourite' spot.

This may be due to a perceived threat – perhaps he has seen another cat come into his garden – or it may just be a case of 'a change is as good as a rest'. Either way, try not to worry too much!

Common behaviour problems

Fright night

Cats are extremely sensitive creatures and are very often terrified by the loud noises and flashes of fireworks and/or thunder storms. Unfortunately fireworks are no longer restricted to one or two nights of the year and are commonly used for all kinds of celebrations including weddings and birthdays. Some cats are so frightened they will panic and run away from home, becoming lost and disorientated or worse, injured in a road traffic accident.

If you have had your cat from being a kitten you may have already tried to desensitize him to loud noises as part of his socialization programme. If not, consider investing in a firework party CD that has been designed specifically to help desensitize cats and dogs to the noise. The idea is that you play it at a low volume during the day when the cat is relaxed and happy. Then you gradually turn up the volume for longer periods until the cat hardly notices the noise at all. Although drug therapy may be useful in the short term, research has shown that the use of desensitizing CDs, combined with facial pheromone plug-in sprays, are the best way to help cats become less fearful. It is also important for the owner to react as normally and calmly as possible. If your cat hides behind the sofa, just allow him to stay there until he feels ready to come out. Constantly holding him and comforting him will only reinforce his fearful reaction and behaviour.

Top Cat Tip

Keep your cat indoors when you are aware that a firework display has been planned in your area. Keep the curtains closed in the room you are in and turn up the volume on your TV or radio to help drown out the noise.

Soiling and spraying

By far the most common behaviour problem reported by vets and animal behaviour counsellors is that of inappropriate indoor soiling. When an adult cat that has always used a litter tray or gone to the toilet outside perfectly happily suddenly starts to soil in the house it can be very distressing for an owner. Sometimes the problem becomes so bad and so stressful that the owner is unable to cope any more and the cat is eventually euthanased. For this reason, it is always best to take early action and seek veterinary advice as soon as possible to rule out a physical cause for the problem.

Once your cat has been given a clean bill of health you can start to tackle the underlying causes. If you feel unable to deal with the problem on your own ask your vet to refer you to a reputable pet behaviour counsellor who will take a very detailed history, visit you and your cat at home and then make an assessment and develop a behaviour modification programme for you to follow.

The first thing that needs to be established is whether the behaviour is inappropriate toileting or territory marking. Marking the territory involves the spraying of urine and depositing of pheromones (chemical markers) from glands in the facial area, tail region and foot pads. French researchers identified over 17 different substances acting as chemical markers in cats.

The use of faeces as a marker is often referred to as middening and typically cats will not cover the faeces up. Territory marking can start if a new cat has moved into the neighbourhood or as a reaction to changes in his environment such as building work or redecoration. Refusal to use a litter tray at all is often a sign of inappropriate toileting problems rather than territory marking.

To try to sort out the problem yourself, however, begin with the litter tray and cat litter. Have these been moved or changed recently? Have you have any building work carried out in the house? Has the cat been disturbed or startled while he was using the litter tray?

It is not always possible to monitor your cat 24 hours a day and know what he gets up to all the time, particularly if you have more than one cat, so even if you think the answers to all of these questions is no, bear in mind that something may have happened that you have no knowledge of.

In any case, reverting back to a cat litter you have tried previously, repositioning the litter tray into a quieter, more private location and possibly investing in a covered litter tray to make the cat feel more secure may help. It is also a good idea to provide a litter tray for every cat in the house.

If the problem of inappropriate soiling continues you may have to go back to basics and try and re-educate the cat. See Chapter 03, page 64 for further tips on re-house training your cat.

Similarly, indoor spraying is often an anxiety reaction. This is why it is important not to shout or physically punish the cat as it will only make him feel more scared and exacerbate the problem. If there is nothing obvious to explain your cat's anxiety, then a pet behaviour counsellor may be able to unravel the origins of the problem. Once this has been determined, the key to modifying this behaviour is to make the cat feel sufficiently at ease in his own home so that he does not feel the need to mark his territory.

Pheromone therapy

The recent development of synthetic facial pheromones (available as a spray, or plug-in diffuser from your vet) has proved very useful in helping to reducing anxiety and the subsequent reaction of indoor spraying. You may have noticed that your cat will often rub his face or cheeks against people and objects. This is an instinctive behaviour, and releases facial pheromones that communicate to the cat that the area is familiar and safe. Synthetic facial pheromone therapy seems to have a calming effect on cats.

Pulling your hair out

Another common behaviour problem reported to counsellors is that of excessive grooming and fur pulling. Although cats groom themselves to keep clean, this is not the only reason. Repeated licking also helps to smooth down the coat, which makes it more efficient at insulating against the cold in winter and cooling them down in the heat of the summer. Tugging out the odd tuft of hair also helps to stimulate the skin glands at the base of the hairs and these secretions are essential in keeping the coat waterproof.

Over grooming (sometimes referred to by behaviourists as displacement grooming) is often a reaction to an anxious situation as the cat tries to calm itself. It is often seen in multi-cat households when there can be a lot of stress and tension between the cats at different times. Just as an anxious owner may start biting her nails when she is feeling nervous, your cat may start to try to calm itself down by grooming. He will also be trying to reinforce his own scent and in the process engage in a pleasurable activity. In some cats the problem becomes so severe that they pull out huge patches of fur.

Once your vet has ruled out a physical cause for the problem it is a case of becoming a cat detective to discover the underlying cause of your cat's anxiety. Remember that cats are extremely sensitive creatures with a highly developed sense of smell, and what is upsetting to them may not be immediately obvious to us. For example, if one cat has been away at the vet for medical treatment and returns home again, you may expect your two cats that have always been firm friends to be delighted to be reunited. However, in some cases the smell of the veterinary surgery on the convalescing cat will be enough to trigger an anxiety reaction in the one who has remained at home. In such a situation the problem may resolve itself within a few days as the smell fades and the cats relax again.

If the situation does not improve your vet may recommend a behaviour modification programme, possibly combined with facial pheromone therapy and/or medication to help relieve the cat's anxiety.

Aggressive behaviour

If you own one cat and he has been well socialized as a kitten you will hopefully not encounter any aggressive behaviour tendencies. If a cat does suddenly show aggression in the form of spitting, hissing or biting when he is handled or picked up then take him for a veterinary check-up to rule out a medical cause. Older cats with hyperthyroidism can develop aggressive behaviour, as can other cats that are in pain.

Cats in multi-cat households are more likely to develop aggressive tendencies. The relationship between various feline members of a household can be tenuous and break down easily.

Signs of aggression

Signs of aggression include:

- Stiffening of the body
- Hissing
- Growling
- Biting
- Refusal to use litter tray
- Changes in sleep or rest patterns
- Flattening of the ears
- Heightened vigilance
- Pupil dilation
- Changes in eating patterns.

Aggression can take different forms. It can occur between cats in the house, cats outside the house, aggression towards the owner and when a queen is protecting her kittens there can be **maternal aggression**.

Outdoor cats are more likely to be involved in **intercat aggression**, and this is primarily about male-to-male competition to try to impress other female cats. Unneutered males are particularly prone to this, which is why neutering is so important. Outdoor cats like to patrol what they consider to be 'their' areas of the neighbourhood and occasionally cross into another cat's territory, resulting in **territorial aggression**.

Another form of aggression that can be very upsetting for an owner is sometimes referred to as **petting aggression**. This is when cats suddenly turn on their owners as they are being stroked or handled. Learning to read your cat's body language and respecting how much he wants to be handled is key to addressing this problem.

Indoor cats are more likely than outdoor cats to exhibit **fear aggression**, simply because they feel unable to escape from what is upsetting or tormenting them. Indoor cats in a multi-cat household are particularly vulnerable to this kind of stress. A good example of bullying behaviour likely to elicit fear aggression is when one cat decides to block a doorway and prevent the other cats from moving freely around the house.

It is also common for frightened cats to demonstrate **displaced aggression**, where they fight with another cat or attack their owner rather than what is scaring them. A good example would be if two indoor cats see a feline intruder enter 'their' garden and feel very threatened by this. Unable to escape or fight, one of the cats may turn on the other, which can be very distressing for owners.

Sometimes it is necessary to separate warring cats then try to reintroduce them again very gradually. When a relationship breaks down to this extent it is better to get professional advice from your vet or a behaviour counsellor who can advise on a management programme.

> **Top Cat Tip**
>
> If you keep more than one cat, ensure that each cat has access to a separate litter tray, feeding station, scratch post and that each cat is able to retreat to a safe area, preferably high up, that will help him to feel safe and secure. Behaviourists like to advise that in a multi-cat household the rule is 'one resource per cat plus one' so that an aggressive cat is unable to deprive another cat of access to anything.

> **Top Cat Tip**
>
> Cat bites can easily become infected so if you find yourself on the receiving end of a scratch or bite, clean the area thoroughly and treat with antiseptics. Always ensure your tetanus vaccinations are kept up to date.

> **Top Cat Tip**
>
> It can be very difficult to stop other cats coming into your garden and upsetting your indoor cats. Obscuring the cat's view of the garden with a sheet of frosted sticky back plastic or frosting spray may help the situation.

Destructive behaviour

Cats are equipped with sharp claws and teeth that can do a lot of damage to the interior of their owner's home. Soft furnishings such as curtains and cushions can be reduced to rags, while tables, chairs and doorposts can be stripped bare. It may be annoying but remember that a cat is not acting out of malice, so there is no point in punishing him for behaving in a way he feels is perfectly normal. Your cat will never think to himself, 'I'm so fed up today I'm going to shred her favourite tablecloth to show her what I think of her!' He will simply be feeling bored and looking for something to entertain him. Heirloom tablecloths and silk scarves are ideal for the job!

Scratching is a normal and essential part of your cat's behaviour patterns. He does it to help remove the outer claw sheath, which helps to sharpen the claws, and also to release some of those pheromones that make him feel relaxed and happy. This is why it is important for every cat to have access to one or more scratching posts. There are many different varieties on the market or you can make your own out of a tree branch. Some cats like the texture of bare wood, while others prefer to dig their claws into sisal or carpet, so experiment to find out what he likes by leaving some areas of the post uncovered. Once you have positioned the scratch post, try to leave it alone as cats do not like their posts being moved around all the time. If you introduce your new kitten to the scratch post he will be unlikely to develop a habit of scratching your furniture.

Boredom is often the cause of destructive behaviour, particularly in indoor cats, which is why it is better to get two kittens rather than one if you are at work all day. Ensure they have plenty of play sessions with you, access to different toys and a climbing/activity centre to keep them entertained. Try leaving them with interactive or puzzle toys to break up the monotony of a long day when you are out of the house.

If your cat develops a preoccupation with something such as wallpaper or a particular piece of furniture, try to distract him away from this as much as you can. A water pistol or plastic spray gun can be a useful thing to keep near by when you are trying to make a behaviour unrewarding. The idea is that if you catch him scratching something you do not want him to do you say 'No' in a loud voice and simultaneously squirt him with the water. This associates the behaviour with an unpleasant experience and should reinforce the verbal command. Take the cat to the scratching post and always praise him enthusiastically when he uses his claws in the correct place. However, be aware that some cats will find being squirted by a water pistol very traumatic and the anxiety can trigger another reaction such as indoor spraying, so seek professional advice if you are worried.

Pica

This condition is sometimes referred to as wool-eating. Pica is a strange behaviour in which cats develop an appetite for non-nutritional substances such as wool, paper, electric cables or rubber. The reason they do this is not fully understood although it is thought that some cats are genetically predisposed and certain environmental stresses such as moving house, or a new cat in the family, may trigger the behaviour. Pica is seen more commonly in young cats, sometimes as young as two to four months, but usually in the first four years of life. There has been a reported increase in this behaviour in Oriental cats, particularly Siamese and Burmese, but it has been observed in many different breeds and is by no means exclusive to Orientals. Early intervention is key to overcoming this problem, which if left untreated can lead to a blockage in the gastro-intestinal tract, and may require surgical intervention.

Your vet will advise on how to treat pica, or may refer your cat to a pet behaviour counsellor. Treatment may include depriving the cat of the substance he craves or only allowing him a small piece of it for a limited time, close supervision and distraction techniques, rewarding acceptable behaviour with a tasty food reward and providing the cat with much more stimulation generally. Changing the cat's diet to a dry high-fibre food may also be recommended.

Common health problems

Despite all your best efforts your cat may develop health problems that require veterinary attention. This can be because of a genetic predisposition, previous medical history, dietary problems or just sheer bad luck. The good news is that veterinary science has developed at such a rate over recent years that more illnesses than ever are treatable and manageable.

Vets see adult cats in their surgeries for a variety of reasons but common problems with middle-age cats include:

- Diabetes
- Feline leukaemia
- Cat flu
- Road accidents
- Behaviour problems
- Poisoning
- Gastric upset
- Dental problems
- Urinary problems such as cystitis
- Skin problems
- Flea allergies
- Ear mites
- Ear and eye infections
- Abscesses as a result of cat fights
- Obesity.

Diabetes

Vets have reported an increase in diabetes mellitus in cats, although it is not known why this is. Heredity and vital infections may be contributory factors but the main reason is thought to be lifestyle, as cats grow fatter and are less active. Signs include increased appetite, thirst, lethargy, increased urination, weight loss and cataracts. It is usually caused when the pancreas is not producing enough insulin and glucose builds up in the bloodstream.

Other associated problems can develop including pancreatitis and Cushing's Disease. Vets initially diagnose diabetes by running a series of tests to record the average blood glucose levels over a period of time (usually 24 hours). Treatment may include an intravenous drip and injections of fast-acting insulin to bring the disease under control and then outpatient treatment as owners are taught how to inject their cat with insulin. Although worried about this initially, most owners cope very well with undertaking this task, particularly when they realize that it is a quick and painless procedure and less troublesome than trying to give tablets.

Many vets will also advise that cats embark on a supervised weight loss programme to improve their prognosis.

Road traffic accidents

Outdoor cats or indoor cats that have escaped are vulnerable to road traffic accidents. Spinal injury and fractured limbs and jaws are very common. If your cat is unfortunate enough to be involved in an accident, try not to panic but do take a minute to telephone your vet before you rush off to the surgery. This will ensure you are going to the right practice, particularly if the accident happened at night and there is an emergency service, and will allow the vet to prepare the examination room for your arrival. Your cat may well require anaesthesia and orthopaedic surgery to try to repair the damage. These procedures are extremely expensive, which is why pet insurance is so useful.

Abscesses

Some cats are more territorial than others and have a tendency to defend what they consider to be their patch. Fight wounds are more likely to occur during the summer months when cats are out for longer periods. Cat bites are often puncture wounds, which heal over and provide an ideal environment for bacteria to multiply and thrive. This infection can cause a weeping, offensive-smelling discharge with an accumulation of pus under the skin. If left untreated this will require draining by the vet and treatment with antibiotics.

Bathe any wound thoroughly in a teaspoonful of salt to a pint of tepid water. Use boiled water that has been allowed to cool down to a temperature the cat will tolerate and find comfortable. If the injury shows signs of infection ask your vet to see the cat and determine whether treatment with antibiotics is necessary.

Feline Lower Urinary Tract Disease (FLUTD)

This is a common problem with cats and affects the entire lower urinary tract including the urethra (tube that carries urine from the bladder out of the body). The most common signs of this are blood in the urine and the cat straining to pass urine. A fresh urine sample is needed to confirm the diagnosis to check for the presence of blood, crystals and bacteria. If an X-ray confirms there is a stone present or the urethra is blocked, surgery will be needed. Appropriate drug therapy and diet are the keys to managing FLUTD and your vet will prescribe a special food for the cat that will alter the conditions in his bladder and help to break up crystals. Encouraging the cat to drink more will help to prevent a recurrence. Your vet will advise on this but adding water to cat food can help, and some cats prefer distilled or filtered water to tap water. You can also try making flavoured ice cubes with prescription food to pop into his water bowl.

Common eye problems

Conjunctivitis

This is an inflammation of the lining surrounding the space around the front surface of the eye, under the eyelids. It can be caused by infection or some sort of irritant and can be associated with another illness such as cat flu. Treatment is usually with antibiotics and/or anti-inflammatory medication.

Uveitis

This is an inflammation of all or part of the iris and retina. There can be corneal damage and raised eye pressure (glaucoma) but this may also be symptomatic of another illness such as feline leukaemia or toxoplasmosis. Uveitis is a painful condition and there may be discharge of blood or pus. The underlying cause of the problem must be treated, and the cat will require medication with anti-inflammatory drugs and painkillers.

Outdoor cats are also at risk of getting a grass seed lodged into their eye, which may cause them discomfort and develop into an infection. Your vet should be able to remove the seed relatively easily and treat any infection with antibiotics.

Poisoning

Ingestion of a toxic substance is a major problem for cats as they are less able to digest this than other species of animal. Researchers have recently discovered that cats are missing a gene that allows them to detect sugars, so if these are present in water they will drink it without knowing and become violently ill.

If you suspect your cat has ingested something poisonous seek urgent veterinary attention.

> **Top Cat Tip**
> Some cats are attracted to the taste of anti-freeze, which can be toxic to them. Ensure all garage doors remain locked and that all cans and bottles are stored safely away.

Giving medications

Cats can be extremely difficult to give tablets to, and if you are uncertain ask your vet or the practice nurse to show you the best way to do this. Plastic pill-givers are available and can be successful, and at least they will protect your fingers! An alternative is to tempt the cat by mixing a crushed tablet into his favourite food or hiding it in something he finds irresistible, such as prawns or a piece of chicken.

> **Top Cat Tip**
> Keeping tablets in the fridge overnight can help to reduce their smell and taste, making them less detectable when you hide them inside a tasty treat.

Out and about

Going into a cattery

If you need to go away on holiday or business and cannot find anyone to look after your cat you may decide to board him in a reputable cattery. The best way to find a good cattery is by asking other cat-owning friends where they take their cats. Your veterinary practice may also be able to recommend an establishment but be aware that good catteries will get fully booked early, particularly at peak times, so make any reservations well in advance to avoid disappointment.

Before you commit to booking into the cattery, however, telephone the owner and arrange to pay a visit. Here is a checklist of things to look out for:

- Does everywhere look clean and tidy?
- Is the establishment licensed with the local authority?
- Who works here and is there a staff presence at all times?
- What type of accommodation are the cats in?
- Is there a slight gap between the cat chalets to help prevent transmission of disease?
- What does the boarding fee include?
- Is heating or administering medications going to involve an extra cost?
- Do all the cats here have vaccination certificates?

- What type of cat litter is used?
- Where is the food preparation area?
- Can the cattery provide the food your cat has?
- Can you bring food for the cat to eat?
- Will they give supplements?
- Will they groom the cats?
- How often are the litter trays changed?
- If you have two cats can they be boarded together in the same chalet?
- What arrangements are made if your cat becomes ill while you are away?
- What insurance do they have?
- What are the cancellation fees?

Once you are satisfied that the cattery is going to suit your cat, make your reservation and if necessary pay a deposit. Find out what time you can deliver and pick up your cat and what is likely to happen if you are unavoidably delayed (for example if your flight is late and you are unable to pick the cat up until the next day).

When you go to the cattery arrive in plenty of time so you can remain calm and help reassure the cat that all is well. Pack his bed, bedding and one of your sweaters or something with your scent on to help him settle. You can also take one or two of his favourite toys and put some treats in the chalet for him.

Most cats settle very well in the cattery so try not to worry about them. You have done everything possible to find a good cattery that will take care of him while you are away. Now it is time to breathe a sigh of relief, relax and enjoy your trip!

Travelling with your cat

Because of recent changes to international legislation and the lifting of quarantine restrictions in the UK and abroad it is now much easier for owners to travel abroad with their pets. When considering whether or not to take your cat with you on holiday you will need to take into account his physical health and age as there are diseases in other countries that your cat will not have encountered before. Your cat's personality type will also help to determine whether or not he will make a suitable travelling companion. Some cats would find being uprooted to a new environment much too stressful and it would be kinder to leave them at home where everything is familiar.

However, if your cat is an outgoing type that tends to be unfazed by almost anything he may well enjoy being with the family on their annual vacation. Of course, you will also need to consider where you are travelling to and the type of holiday you have planned; a rented cottage in the south of France may be ideal, whereas a package holiday in a crowded, noisy seaside resort in the middle of August would be totally impractical. You can always ask your vet for advice on whether or not to take your cat if you feel undecided.

> **Top Cat Tip**
>
> If you are planning to travel overseas with your cat, start preparing early as it is a slow process and it can take several months to prepare the paperwork and complete the necessary tests.

It is always wise to check the importation requirements of any country you are travelling to as they will all vary slightly. Although some countries may allow you to leave the country of origin, if you do not have the correct paperwork you will not be allowed to re-enter. In the USA, contact the US Department of Agriculture (USDA) – see Taking it Further – for up-to-date travel requirements. Most countries require a current rabies vaccination and in the USA you need a US Interstate and International Certificate. Your vet can advise on the current regulations, tests and certificates required.

Pet Travel Scheme checklist
To travel abroad with you, your cat will need:

- **To be microchipped.**
- **A rabies vaccination** – One injection will usually provide sufficient immunity.
- **A blood test** – Your cat will need to have a blood sample taken three to four weeks after he has had his rabies vaccine. This is to check that he has developed antibodies to the disease. If he does not pass this test he will be unable to travel until he has had another rabies injection and a positive antibody test.
- **A pet passport** – Once your cat has a positive blood test result he will be issued with a passport. In the UK cats can only travel six months *after* a successful blood test, which is why it is so important to arrange the blood test at least six months before you travel, otherwise he will not be allowed back. After six months, provided your cat is up to date with his vaccines, he will be allowed to travel with you as often as you like.

- **Treatment for ticks and tapeworms** – 24–48 hours before returning to the UK, your cat must be treated for ticks and tapeworms by an approved vet, who will then sign his passport.
- **Approved journey home** – You must travel through a recognized route or port when you come home, so check your route first. At the port or airport your cat will be scanned to check his microchip matches his passport.

Stay at home vacations

The tourism industry now recognizes that many people like to vacation at home with their cat and cat-friendly accommodation is widely available. The best places tend to get fully booked very early, particularly during high season, so book ahead to avoid disappointment.

A portable crate is the best way to travel with your cat. He can sleep in it and safely stay inside if you visit friends or a restaurant. You can also store his toys, blankets and bed inside.

Top ten tips to ensure that your cat stays healthy and happy

1 Give him a routine. Cats are not fond of surprises and they like to know what time they are going to be fed, when you are going to get up, play with them, let them out, allow them back in, etc. Establishing a routine will help to make your cat feel secure and confident.

2 Provide him with a comfy bed. It can be a cardboard box with a cushion and a blanket inside but take care where you position it. Location is everything! Older cats will appreciate their beds being next to the fireplace or a warm radiator. The best place is in a quiet, draught-free corner.

3 Take him for his annual check-up. OK, he might not seem over the moon about the idea but you will be ensuring that he is happy and healthy, which has to be a good thing.

4 Allow him to be a cat. Too much love and being over protective can actually be a bad thing. If your cat never gets the opportunity to express his natural feline behaviours he will find this very frustrating. Do not worry if he is climbing onto high shelves or wobbling along the top of a fence, let him get on with it rather than continually trying to rescue him from what you perceive to be threatening situations.

5 Food, glorious food! Your cat will be extremely happy if you provide him with a well-balanced diet that consists of the best quality cat food you can afford.

6 Treats! Everyone loves the odd treat and cats are no exception. In particular, they love a nice piece of fish, chicken or a fresh, fat prawn. You can buy commercially prepared cat treats but take these into account when calculating your cat's daily calorie allowance. Otherwise you will be wondering why your cat has suddenly put on lots of extra weight and is looking decidedly unhappy!

7 Playtime. Take time every day to play with your cat. You can both really enjoy this time together. Try to ensure he has at least two interactive play sessions with you and, if possible, three. They only have to last ten minutes or so, but in doing so you will ensure he remains as fit and active as possible throughout his life.

8 Time out. Take a few minutes every day just to sit with your cat, stroke him and talk to him and this will help to strengthen the bond and the relationship you have.

9 Grooming. This is a great way to make your cat happy, provided you take your time and make the entire experience as relaxed and fun as possible. For this reason, do not rush through it when you are trying to get out to work, but instead do it when you are not in a hurry, such as when you are settled down to watch one of your favourite soaps on the television. Make this a part of your daily routine.

10 Give as well as take. When you are very busy in your everyday life it is sometimes easy to ignore your cat. OK, you may provide food and water for him and throw the odd toy but very often he is left to his own devices. Be aware of his emotional needs and respect the fact that he needs and deserves some attention from you at certain times. Research shows that owners who allow their cats to come to them to initiate contact have a stronger relationship with them than when the owner always insists on initiating and ending social contact.

Did you know?

For the ultimate in entertaining cats, you can now buy videos and DVDs that have been filmed especially for them! So, if you have to go out to work you could set the recorder to come on and play a selection of squirrels, birds and chipmunks in action. You can also buy films of fish swimming in an aquarium!

Ten ways to be a happy owner

1 The first step to being a happy owner is to have a contented cat. Whether he lives indoors or has access to outdoors, provided he has enough exercise, mental stimulation, companionship and a good diet, he will be a happy and relaxed feline. This will make your life a whole lot easier, and mean you should not be dealing with a stressed or anxious cat that is exhibiting behaviour problems.

2 Learn to relax. Cats are like emotional sponges and will pick up on and mirror how their owners are feeling. If you are tense and angry, if there are a lot of arguments in your home or you are anxious about something, the chances are your cat will recognize this and react accordingly. This is something to consider if you think your cat is 'misbehaving' in some way. In fact, he may be doing his best to cope with a situation that is beyond his control. So, take a few deep breaths and learn to relax. That way, both you and your cat will be a lot happier!

3 Remember that you are the head of your own household. As much as you love your cat, if you allow him to assume the responsibility of this role by pandering to his every need and giving in to every little demand that he makes you will risk creating a very possessive and over-dependent cat. Taken to extremes this will mean you are rarely able to leave the house, for fear of what mess and destruction you will come home to! If you think you are over-attached to your cat, you need to learn to ignore him occasionally, by not giving eye contact, or any physical or verbal interaction no matter how much he tries to get your attention.

4 Seek early advice if your cat develops behaviour or physical problems. Do not think you are failing as an owner in some way, or be too embarrassed to seek help. Sometimes professional advice is the best way forward and the earlier that help is sought, the sooner a problem can be sorted out.

5 Introduce any changes to your home as gradually as you can. Cats are very sensitive to change, even interior décor or moving the furniture can upset some of them! If you are expecting a baby or getting married, introduce the cat to your partner or bring some baby things into the home well before the expected date of arrival. This way you can continue to enjoy your cat and your new circumstances without worrying too much.

6 Take up bird watching! If you have an indoor cat you can keep him entertained for hours by putting a bird table near to the window. This way both you and he can enjoy watching the antics of those feathered friends without risk of him injuring them. Site bird tables carefully if you have an outdoor cat or other cats are in the neighbourhood.

7 Spend time finding a good boarding kennel and creating a list of people you can call to look after the cat in an emergency. There is nothing worse than being delayed getting home from work and worrying that your cat is stuck in the house with nothing to eat. Knowing you can rely on someone to help you out occasionally will really help you to relieve the stress.

8 Volunteer! If you have an hour or two to spare why not offer your time and services to a local cat charity. Helping other needy cats will give you a great sense of personal satisfaction and you will meet lots of interesting people and make other cat-loving friends as well.

9 Your cat brings you so much pleasure that it can be very rewarding to see other people enjoy him too. If your cat is a very placid type who enjoys meeting lots of different people he may be suitable for use as a therapy cat. In the UK, the organization Pets As Therapy has cats as well as dogs that regularly visit older people and children in hospitals, schools and residential homes. This can be a fun way of helping others and making new friends. For more information contact the PAT website at: www.pat.co.uk

10 Be a copy cat! You may have noticed that, in general, cats are very contented creatures. So, to be a really happy owner, why not take a few tips from your cat? Start by learning to look after yourself, eat well, sleep lots, never be afraid to make a fool of yourself and spend as much time as possible indulging in some serious grooming and pampering! For more hints and tips on lessons your cat can teach you, see page Chapter 06.

05

owning an OAP
(old age puss)

In this chapter you will learn:
- about health and behaviour problems
- about nutrition for OAPs
- how to cope with the final goodbye.

Cats are now living longer than ever and this is undoubtedly because of improvements in veterinary medicine, nutritional science and greater knowledge of feline behaviour. With so many books and magazines devoted to caring for cats, owners are also much more educated and there is no doubt that a healthy diet and regular preventative health care will really help the cat to enjoy his senior years.

The longevity of cats is also due to the fact that many more owners choose to get their cats neutered. This helps to prevent the development of life-threatening diseases such as mammary cancer in female cats and infectious diseases such as feline immunodeficiency virus (FIV), which is primarily spread when an infected cat bites another. Neutering reduces the likelihood of a cat roaming and becoming involved in a fight with another cat, or getting injured in a road traffic accident.

Did you know?

Research over the past decade shows that in the USA 15 per cent more cats are now living beyond the age of ten years. It is thought that the figure is similar in the UK.

It is important to remember that all cats are individuals and the ageing process is going to affect them in different ways. Just like humans, some cats age better than others, and one ten-year-old cat may look older than his 20-year-old friend. Get to know your cat, how he normally looks and behaves, so that you can assess any changes that are occurring. Often it is an owner's hunch that something is 'just not quite right' that is the best indication that all is not well.

Senior health clinics

Once a cat has reached the age of ten he is considered to be in his senior or geriatric years. Many vets now provide senior pet clinics and if your practice does so, take advantage of this service.

Senior pet clinics are usually offered twice a year and will involve an extended consultation, where the vet examines the cat's heart, lungs, joints, skin, teeth, etc. They may also take a blood sample to check how well the cat's internal organs are functioning, as well as the levels of thyroid hormones. You can also expect the cat's blood pressure to be taken, possibly a urine sample to check for diabetes, and plenty of advice on how to feed and manage your old age puss. These health-screening clinics are very useful in helping to detect any problems very early on, so that treatment has a greater chance of success.

How old is your cat?

It used to be said that one year in a cat's life is the equivalent of seven in human years but this is not really accurate. Kittens grow and develop very quickly in the first year or two but then ageing slows down somewhat. At the age of one year, a cat is probably the equivalent of a 15-year-old teenager, and after that the ageing process slows so that one year in a cat's life is about four years in a human's. Therefore when a cat is three years old, a human would be 28, when the cat is seven a human is 44 and when a cat is 11 a human is 60. As in humans, 60 years of age is by no means considered very elderly. By the time your cat is 20 years of age, he is probably the equivalent of a 96-year-old, so entitled to the respect of a very senior citizen!

figure 7 your old age puss will enjoy more naps over the years

---

Did you know?

According to the *Guinness Book of World Records* a cat called Granpa was the world's longest-living cat. Granpa died on 1 April 1998, aged 34 years, two months (and four hours!). The previous record of 34 years and one day was set by a tabby cat from England in 1957.

Physiological changes to expect

You may notice that your cat slows down and becomes less active as he grows older. He may sleep more and generally take things easier. This could in part be due to joint problems such as arthritis and the fact that moving has become more difficult or painful for him, so he avoids this as much as possible. His muscle tone will reduce and this also contributes to an inability to move as well as he did in his youth.

There could be a change in his appetite, and he may eat more or less than normal. If this happens, consult your vet for advice as it could indicate an underlying problem. Senior cats often develop a diminished sense of smell and taste, which can affect appetite.

Dental disease is very common in elderly cats but there are special senior diets available to help exercise the gums and remove some of the tartar that is building up on the teeth. Cats that have lost their teeth may find eating dried food difficult, and a change to a softer, moist food may be recommended.

As older cats tend to utilize the food they eat less efficiently than younger cats, they often lose weight and some become constipated. Senior diets contain higher levels of fat and easily digestible energy sources.

You may also notice that your older cat undergoes something of a personality change (although this is not always the case). Some cats become calm and tranquil with old age, while others become downright grumpy and demanding! Thankfully it would seem that by far the most likely change is for the cat to become more loving and affectionate, seeking reassurance from his owner. If a cat does change in personality very suddenly there is probably a medical reason for this, so get him checked as soon as possible to ensure that he is not in pain or learning to adjust to physiological changes such as blindness or deafness that make him a little anxious.

In addition, a cat who was never happier exploring the great outdoors may suddenly decide life as a housecat is much more appealing. His reluctance to go out may in part be due to a thinning of his coat which is making him more susceptible to the cold and rain.

Older cats are prone to the following health problems:

• Arthritis
• Loss of sight or hearing

- Diabetes
- Kidney disease
- Urinary tract problems
- Dental disease
- Thyroid malfunction
- Liver failure
- Heart disease
- Tumours
- Senile dementia.

The good news is that veterinary medicine has developed so much that many new treatments are available to help cure and control the above diseases. Owners need not be afraid that a diagnosis will signal an automatic death sentence.

Older cats and vaccines

As a cat becomes older some people question the necessity for continuing booster vaccinations and certainly some vets agree that the cat may have built up sufficient immunity. However, there are just as many vets who recommend that booster vaccination continues as the theory is that a cat's immune system deteriorates as he grows older, making him more vulnerable and susceptible to infections. The best advice is to chat this through with your vet and find out what his vaccination policy is, then you can make a decision.

Common health problems in older cats

As a cat grows older some organs and bodily systems become less efficient. Older cats can develop one or more conditions, and this can complicate the diagnosis and treatment.

Kidney disease

It is very common for older cats to show signs of chronic or long-term kidney damage. Damage to the cells that flush toxins out of the blood for removal in the cat's urine is a normal part of the ageing process. The most common cause of kidney disease in older cats is chronic interstitial nephritis, a degenerative change due to general wear and tear of the kidneys and the replacement of normal kidney cells with scar tissue. The kidneys have a lot of spare capacity and the symptoms of kidney disease will only present themselves when over three-quarters of the kidneys have been lost.

Signs of kidney disease include:

- **Increased urination and thirst** – Healthy cats do not drink excessively, so if you notice that your cat is now going to the water bowl, tap or garden pond more than usual it is worth informing your vet
- **Decreased appetite** – As kidney disease progresses the cat may develop mouth ulcers, making him reluctant to eat (particularly dried food)
- **Halitosis** – A build-up of toxins means that many cats with kidney disease have bad breath.

While it is not possible to cure long-term kidney disease, it is possible to control it provided the owner is very committed to this. Cats are given a combination of fluid therapy if they are dehydrated, a low-protein diet and drug therapy. Early use of drugs that block the activity of hormones that cause fluid retention and a rise in blood pressure have been shown to significantly improve the lives of cats with kidney disease. Such cats lose vitamins through their kidneys and therefore vets sometimes recommend water-soluble vitamin B supplements. Cats with kidney disease need to be closely monitored, so vets will regularly check their weight, blood and blood pressure as well as review their diet.

Diabetes

Diabetes mellitus (which is sometimes referred to as sugar diabetes) is becoming more common in cats, although the reason for this is not yet fully understood. It is similar to the diabetes suffered by humans and it is thought that genetic disposition, viral infections, diet and lifestyle may all contribute to the development of the disease.

Diabetes occurs when there is insufficient insulin in the body. Insulin is a hormone that maintains blood sugar (glucose) at its optimum level for good health. A lack of insulin results in a build-up of sugar in the blood, which eventually starts to appear in the urine.

Signs of diabetes:

- Increased thirst and urination
- Weight loss
- Fatigue and lethargy
- Increased appetite
- Cataracts.

Seek veterinary advice if your cat exhibits any or all of the above symptoms as left untreated the condition can be fatal. If your vet suspects a diagnosis of diabetes he will arrange to measure the cat's blood glucose levels, probably as an in-patient over a 24-hour period. In doing so he will note if and when the cat experiences a 'hypo', which is the term commonly used to describe when blood glucose levels have dropped too low.

Once a diagnosis has been confirmed, treatment can begin. In severe cases this may require an intravenous drip and injections of fast-acting insulin. Once the cat has been stabilized he will probably be allowed home and treated as an out-patient. If the cat is overweight, veterinary staff will probably advise and support the owner as they attempt to reduce the cat's weight with a low calorie diet. If your cat is lucky and the condition is caught early enough, weight reduction may be enough to control the problem although glucose levels will still need to be monitored. Special prescription foods are available for diabetic cats and your vet will advise you on how much and how often to feed, depending on the type of insulin being used.

Owners will be taught how to inject their cats with insulin (probably twice daily) and generally speaking this is less stressful and more effective for the cat than trying to give oral medication. The needles are incredibly fine and once an owner has overcome his initial shock at administering an injection, they are very quick and painless.

Glucose monitoring is usually done through urine and special cat litters are now available to make the job much easier.

Arthritis

Although it is more common for dogs to develop arthritis than cats, when it does occur it can be very debilitating. Feline Progressive Polyarthritis affects different joints and deteriorates as the disease progresses. Wear and tear of the thin layer of cartilage that protects the surface of the bone causes damage to the joints. Without the normal protection, joints become inflamed and swollen and the condition is very painful. Although the disease mainly affects elderly cats, those that are young or middle aged can also be affected. There are many different types of and causes for arthritis, but it is important to act quickly if you suspect your cat is developing problems. Do not be tempted to embark on any human medications or cod liver oil supplements. Cod liver oil is rich in Vitamin A, which will accumulate in the liver and cause problems in the future.

Signs of joint disease:

- Stiffness, especially after resting or sleeping
- Reluctance to play or exercise
- Limping, particularly in cold, wet weather
- Grumpiness at being handled
- Licking or biting at a painful area.

If a cat is overweight, embarking on a restricted-calorie weight-loss programme as recommended by your vet will undoubtedly be very helpful.

Although arthritic cats may be reluctant to move, prolonged periods of immobility will exacerbate the problem. Encouraging them to participate in gentle exercise sessions, little and often, will help to loosen the joints and keep them more mobile and pain free. Your vet may also recommend the application of warm compresses and massage which can help your cat to feel more comfortable.

Drug treatment with non-steroidal anti-inflammatories (NSAIDS) or corticosteroids may be advised. Supplements with glucosamine and chondroitin have enjoyed remarkable success. Chrondroitin helps to block the enzymes that break down cartilage and glucosamine helps the body to rebuild new cartilage. When used in conjunction with each other the duration and dosage of conventional drug treatment may well be reduced, thus lessening the risk of side-effects from prolonged steroidal treatment.

There are a few practical things you can do to help your arthritic cat enjoy life more. Begin by positioning his litter trays, food and water bowls where they are all easily accessible and perhaps putting an extra litter tray and water bowl down for him so that he does not have to move quite as far to get to them each time. Changing his litter box to one with lower sides so that it is easier for him to get in and out of may also help him to manage better.

If your cat enjoys sleeping on a favourite sofa, chair or sunny windowsill you can put steps or ramps close by to help him climb up and down.

Grooming may also become more difficult for an arthritic cat. Twisting the neck round can be painful and so your cat will appreciate some help this department if you give him a gentle, daily grooming session.

Hyperthyroidism

Hyperthyroidism (an over-active gland) is almost exclusively seen in cats over the age of seven years. It occurs when overactive thyroid glands (found in the base of the neck) produce too much of the hormone. The thyroid helps to control the cat's metabolic rate and when it dysfunctions it can cause a variety of unpleasant symptoms and associated complications for the cat.

Signs of hyperthyroidism:

- Increased appetite
- Drinking more than usual
- Irritability
- Weight loss
- Restlessness
- Hyperactivity.

Thankfully, when diagnosed early enough hyperthyroidism is usually treatable and can sometimes be cured. Your vet will diagnose the condition through blood tests, physical examination and possibly a scan.

There are various treatment options available and your vet will advise on the most suitable, whether this is drug therapy, surgical intervention or radio-iodine therapy.

Behaviour in old age

Older cats can develop changes to behaviour as they learn to cope with various disabilities. For example, joint stiffness may make grooming themselves more difficult, while reduced muscle tone and thinning of the coat may cause them to change their normal sleeping place in favour of a softer, warmer spot. Inability to groom can also be one of the signs of kidney disease, due to the development of mouth ulcers and fatigue.

Many diseases of old age, including the development of tumours or hyperthyroidism, can cause behavioural changes such as mood change or irritability. Vets are also now aware that chemical changes in the brain of an older cat can cause imbalances, which affect behaviour. As the cat ages, the normal balance of various neurotransmitters, including dopamine, serotonine and nor-epinephrine is disrupted. This can affect mood and behaviour and collectively is referred as cognitive dysfunction. Reduced blood supply may also deprive the brain of oxygen, compromising its ability to function.

Signs of cognitive dysfunction in the Old Age Puss include:

- **Sleep disruption** – Often more frequent but less heavy sleep patterns are noted.
- **Hypervocalization** – Your previously quiet cat may suddenly become very vocal and noisy, often at night and sometimes for no apparent reason.
- **Disorientation** – This confusion can result in some incontinence, if a cat is unable to find a litter tray.
- **Non-responsiveness** – A cat may no longer show recognition or interact with his owners in the way he used to when younger.

Cognitive dysfunction is an area of pharmacology that is being studied a great deal at present. New drugs are being developed to correct chemical imbalances and improve the blood supply to the brain, making a cat's senior years much more pleasant.

Caring for the older cat

As your cat ages he may need and appreciate a little more help. In particular, stiffness and joint pain can make grooming problematic so even if you have never had to do this before, a daily brush and comb may be required. It may be worth reviewing the grooming equipment you have used over the years and, if necessary, investing in some new, softer brushes and a chamois grooming mitt that will be gentler on sensitive skin and kinder around the joints.

This daily grooming will help you to check your cat for any unusual lumps, bumps or skin problems that may require medical attention. Most older cats are keen to spend as much time as possible with their owners and really enjoy all the extra fuss and pampering they are being given.

Older cats are much more prone to dental disease, so continue to brush his teeth and check the mouth and gums for signs of inflammation or ulcers. Halitosis can be a sign of kidney disease and checking the mouth gives you an opportunity to assess and monitor any changes.

Some cats with mobility problems experience a little more difficulty in keeping themselves clean at the back end. If this becomes a problem you can help by trimming away any long hair in this area (using round-ended scissors), and cleaning with damp cotton wool and tepid water. It is also possible to buy disposable wipes for cats that you can use to help keep them clean and sweet smelling.

Claw clipping

Claw clipping may become necessary as your cat ages (see Plate 13). Over the years the claws are less able to retract and more likely to become trapped in material such as the carpet or cushions. Your cat may also be less able or inclined to reach up and use his usual scratching post to keep his claws in good condition and if the claws become so long that they grow into the pad, it is very painful for the cat. If you have never had to clip his claws before and are uncertain, you can always ask your vet or practice nurse to demonstrate how it is done.

How to clip claws

Only use clippers specifically designed for cats' claws to give your cat a manicure. For the front claws, it is easiest to sit with the cat on your lap, facing away from you. Then lean forwards a little and bring your arms up so that your body weight and arm position can help to prevent the cat from wriggling about too much. If a cat is very restless you can use your forearm to hold his head out of the way while you clip.

Your aim is to trim the white tip, which will not hurt the cat as it is dead tissue. Only clip from the top to the bottom and avoid going down to the pinkish quick as this contains nerves and will cause pain and a strong reaction from the cat if you cut it! If you do accidentally nick this quick it will probably bleed, but do not panic. Simply apply pressure with a pad of cotton wool until the bleeding stops.

If the cat is calm you can keep him in the same position to clip his claws on the hind legs, but this time without leaning forwards. If he is very restless you may find that wrapping him in a towel or blanket and exposing one claw at a time will help restrain him enough for you to get the job done.

> **Top Cat Tip**
> Avoid cutting away at the sides of the claws or you will cause the nail to splinter.

Hairballs

Because cats are constantly grooming themselves they tend to swallow a lot of dead hair. Most of the hair is eliminated through the digestive system in the cat's faeces but because hair is not particularly digestible, some of it may remain and form a dense ball or matt, which the cat then gets rid of by vomiting. Anyone who has ever heard the alarming sounding noise of a cat gagging or retching as it tries to vomit a hairball will know how unforgettable and unmistakable a noise this is!

Cats with hairballs can also experience loss of appetite, swollen stomach, diarrhoea or constipation. Hairballs can be more common in older cats and problems arise if the cat is unable either to vomit them up or eliminate them in faeces. Left untreated, hairballs can cause an impaction in the digestive tract and vets have been known to remove enormous hairballs the size of a soccer ball from the stomachs of cats. Impaction is a serious problem and requires urgent medical intervention, so contact your vet if you suspect this.

Regular grooming, particularly of longhair cats, can help to prevent the problem from recurring but there is no doubt that some cats are more prone to them than others. Your vet may also recommend lubricating the cat's digestive tract by administering some kind of oil that will help the hair pass through more easily.

A high-fibre diet or fibre supplement may also help with a chronic hairball problem and there are also diets that have been developed specifically to help the condition.

Feeding the older cat

You may find that it becomes necessary to adjust your cat's diet and food intake as he grows older. As healthy older cats tend to drink less water, a moist diet with a higher water content is often preferable to dry food to ensure they are getting enough fluids. Remember, though, it is important to introduce any changes to diet very gradually to avoid gastric upset.

Research shows 70 per cent of older cats experience some form of dental disease. Because of this older cats may also find wet food easier to eat than dried food, particularly if there are missing or broken teeth that make crunching difficult. If your cat has always really enjoyed dried food you can still offer him a few as treats. If he can manage to eat biscuits these will help to exercise his mouth and gums and prevent the build-up of plaque. Some cats with hardly any teeth still manage to eat dry cat food quite happily!

As usual, your cat should always have easy access to fresh drinking water but watch him as he drinks to ensure that he can find and get to his water easily. If he has an arthritic spine and experiences difficulty or pain when moving his neck he may appreciate having his food and water bowls on stands so that they are higher up and he has to bend his head down less in order to reach them.

Thankfully, now that cats are living so much longer, pet food manufacturers are spending a lot of time and money researching the dietary needs of the older puss. Because of this there are now many senior diet foods available that have been developed specifically to cater for their changing nutritional requirements.

The older a cat becomes the less efficient his body is at utilizing the food he eats. This is the reason why older cats need a diet that is higher in easily digested energy, which is why senior diets contain higher levels of fat. They are usually slightly lower in protein and phosphorus, to help prevent kidney disease.

Research shows that antioxidants can help to slow down the ageing process, and most senior diets are therefore rich in these. They also contain an amino acid known as L-carnitine, which has been shown to be beneficial to older cats. Older cats can be prone to developing urinary problems caused by the build-up of a crystal known as oxalates, which tend to make the urine acidic. Senior diets are designed to produce urine that is more alkaline than in younger cats.

> **Top Cat Tip**
> Adding a few drops of hot water to your cat's food to produce a little gravy can help to mulch dry food and make it more palatable.

If your senior cat is suffering from any type of medical condition, there is probably a prescription diet available from your vet specifically designed to help manage this. A good example is the low protein/phosphorus diet developed to help manage kidney disease.

> **Top Cat Tip**
> Offer a small tin of canned tuna only as an occasional treat. If fed regularly it can lead to finicky eating or nutritional deficiencies.

As the cat's sense of taste and smell diminishes with age, the less able he becomes to recognize and enjoy his food. So when feeding older cats, the diet needs to be more palatable than for kittens or middle-aged cats.

> **Top Cat Tip**
> Remove your cat's food from the refrigerator about 20 minutes before you intend to feed him. This will bring the food up to room temperature and your cat may be able to smell and enjoy it more. Heating the food up for a few seconds in the microwave may also help to make it more appealing.

Complementary therapies

More owners than ever are interested in a holistic approach to caring for their cats and look towards complementary therapies to help them recover from illness or enjoy life more. It is difficult to state how effective these therapies are but, as the name suggests, they should always be used to complement conventional medicine and not be used as an alternative.

Unfortunately, the complementary therapy industry is largely unlicensed and poorly monitored so that many unqualified people claim to be practitioners of all kinds of treatments. Some of these practitioners, despite having the animals' best interests at heart, very often do more harm than good as they do not have the necessary anatomical, physiological and scientific knowledge to diagnose and treat ailments. In the UK only qualified veterinary surgeons are legally able to treat an animal, and it is important to seek the advice of your vet before embarking on any complementary therapy. While some vets remain sceptical, others do recognize homoeopathy, herbal medicine and acupuncture as viable treatments and specialize in these areas. You can ask your vet to be referred for a second opinion if you would like some advice on these therapies.

The field of complementary therapy is huge and entire books have been written on the subject. Here is an insight into some of the most popular therapies that are available for cats.

Acupuncture and acupressure

Acupuncture is probably one of the most widely known and popular of the healing therapies but must always be carried out by a vet. Based on the principles of Traditional Chinese Medicine (TCM), it involves the insertion of fine needles into specific points of the body known as meridians, in an effort to help regulate the 'life force' that flows through the organs. TCM practitioners believe that an imbalance in the flow of vital energy (yin and yang) can cause acute or chronic disease. In traditional acupuncture the practitioner will insert needles into various sites, and then gently stimulate the needles either manually or electronically. It is a painless procedure and the benefits are said to include:

- Stimulation of the body's natural defence systems.
- Effective for a wide range of problems, including chronic diseases.
- No side-effects.
- Useful for conditions that are unresponsive to medications such as Feline Immunodeficiency Virus (FIV) and Feline Leukaemia (FeLV).
- Can be used when surgery is not a feasible option.
- Fast results, either immediately or within a couple of sessions.

A wide variety of conditions are treated with acupuncture. These include skin conditions, joint problems, infertility, respiratory disorders, allergies and pain relief. Some vets use lasers instead of needles, particularly if a cat is very nervous.

Did you know?

There is evidence that animals have been treated with acupuncture for many thousands of years. It is known that government veterinarians treated livestock in the Chow Dynasty (2303 BC). Since then, it has been practised continuously in China. In the USA the National Association of Veterinary Acupuncture (NAVA) has pioneered the treatment of animals, while in the UK The Association of British Veterinary Acupuncturists (ABVA) is working to gain recognition for this therapy.

Acupressure massage is also part of the TCM system and can be carried out by owners, but it is advisable to have a chat with your vet before you embark on any treatment. Acupressure works in a similar way to acupuncture, but is non-invasive as it does not involve the use of any needles. Hands and fingers are used to stimulate the acupuncture points and balance the flow of Chi energy in the body. Because cats love to be touched, they often find acupressure very calming and relaxing.

Aromatherapy

This involves the use of highly diluted essential oils extracted from aromatic plants to enhance health and beauty. Extracts from all parts of the plants are used including the leaves, petals and roots. Often described as the life force of the plants, they can be highly volatile substances and up to 100 times more concentrated on extraction than in the plant. With cats they are inhaled, massaged, or used as vapours and work on the olfactory system (sense of smell) to affect different parts of the body. The cats are allowed to sniff and choose their own oils from a selection laid out by the practitioner and should never be forced to sniff or lick an essential oil.

A degree of caution is necessary because cats are extremely sensitive creatures and unable to synthesize or break down substances as well as humans or other animals. For this reason, specially diluted forms of the oils are usually used on cats and it is advisable to consult a qualified aromatherapist who has had experience of working with cats. A variety of physical and emotional ailments are said to benefit from treatment with aromatherapy.

Kinesiology

Kinesiology also embraces the theories of Chinese medicine and is often used by aromatherapists to assess energy flow throughout the body. The practitioner will isolate the muscles that relate to various acupuncture meridians then test their strength to see if there are any physical or emotional imbalances. Some practitioners claim to be able to do this using only a sample of the cat's hair.

Bach flower remedies

Harley Street doctor Edward Bach created these gentle, flower-based plant remedies in the 1930s. He recognzed the importance of spiritual and emotional wellbeing and developed them to help correct emotional imbalances and replace negative emotions with positive ones. Cats are very emotional animals, capable of expressing love, fear, happiness, stress and grief and it is claimed that they respond well to flower remedies. As cats tend to act as their owners' emotional mirrors, they will pick up on any stress or anxiety the owner is experiencing and then reflect this back. It is safe for the owner and cat to share a remedy to help overcome any negative feelings. Cats are sometimes reluctant to drink water with remedies in as they are very fussy but it may be possible to put a drop on their paws, so they can lick it off and absorb the remedy that way. Some owners find that Bach Rescue Remedy, a combination of several flower remedies developed for use in an emergency situation, is very useful if a cat is traumatized by a particular situation such as a visit to the vet or the cattery. Bach Flower Remedies are available from many health shops or can be purchased via the Internet.

Other companies have launched flower remedies and it is now possible to buy essences that have been specially developed for use on pets.

> ### Top Cat Tip
>
> Be wary about putting anything onto your cat's coat that may adversely affect his grooming habits. Cats can experience strong reactions to some chemicals that do not affect other pets. In particular, tea tree oil, which is often viewed as a natural and therefore harmless anti-bacterial substance, can be very potent and toxic to cats if it has not been diluted sufficiently.

Homoeopathy

This is an extremely popular therapy with owners, both for use on themselves and their cats. Homoeopathy is based on the principle of treating like with like. Depending on the cat's ailment a substance, when given in minute homoeopathic quantities, can help to ease or cure the symptoms when they are produced in the body by some other cause, like illness or disease. This is sometimes referred to as a 'hair of the dog' treatment and is basically how a vaccine works. Homoeopathy is generally considered to be a very safe therapy, as the treatments have been diluted down to miniscule levels and the dose will be the same for a cat or an elephant – it is how often the remedy is taken that matters.

Owners who visit a homoeopathic vet should expect to be involved a long history-taking session prior to the cat being physically examined.

Homoeopathy is used to treat a wide range of ailments. For further information you can visit the website of the British Association of Homeopathic Veterinary Surgeons at www.bahvs.com, or the American Holistic Vetinary Medical Association at www.ahvma.org.

Herbal medicine

Some vets chosse to specialize in herbal medicine. Despite the fact that many people consider non-conventional treatments to be safer, herbal medicine must be used with caution. Cats do not metabolize drugs in the same way that humans or other animals do and their livers lack an enzyme necessary to break down some of the substances found in herbal medicines. Because a cat is unable to get rid of the substance they can develop liver damage. For this reason never treat a cat with herbal medicines yourself, but always consult a qualified vet who has a special interest in this field.

T-Touch

TTEAM, an acronym for Tellington-Touch Every Animal Method, was devised by Canadian practitioner, Linda Tellington Jones. The exercises (see Plate 14) involve a series of very slow, gentle, circular movements performed all over the cat's body and the benefits are said to be wide ranging including helping to relax them, increase circulation, aid healing and improve the bond that exists between owner and cat. It can be a very useful technique in helping cats that are difficult to handle to understand that contact with a human can be an enjoyable experience.

Practitioners claim that the circular movements help to awaken and rejuvenate cells 'a little like turning on the electric light switch' in the body. As well as hands, practitioners use a variety of tools to help them deal with cats, including stroking with some kind of 'wand' such as a paintbrush or feather, which allows them to continue making contact while keeping at a safe distance. Even the most difficult cats seem to enjoy the attention and soon appear perfectly relaxed and happy throughout.

Sometimes wraps are use to help a cat to become accustomed to being lifted. These are applied with a series of gentle feels and releases to help teach the cat that being contained and constricted is not something for them to worry about.

If you are interested in finding out more about TTEAM, there are many books, workshops and videos available on the subject. For more information you can also visit www.tillefarm.co.uk or www.tteam-ttouch.com.

How to enhance and enrich your OAP's life

As your cat matures into a senior citizen there are many little things you can do that will help to make a big difference to his creature comforts.

- Be aware that as your cat grows older and his joints stiffen he will slow down. Although it is good to encourage him to engage in a little gentle exercise, he will not be as inclined to roam around the house and seek his owner out as freely as he used to. Do not allow him to become isolated from other pets or family members, spending hours on end by himself. Put a cosy bed in a warm place in the heart of the home and encourage your cat to spend time there when you are at home so that he can see and feel he is part of the family.
- Have a look around your home and see if there are any little things you can do to help keep your cat mobile and able to enjoy life. For example, you could place boxes or ramps in strategic positions so that he is able to climb up on to a favourite sunny windowsill or chair.

- Stairs can become a problem for elderly cats to negotiate and they may have difficulty getting to a downstairs litter tray in time. For this reason, place a litter tray upstairs as well as in his normal spot downstairs. Put a water bowl upstairs as well, to encourage him to drink.

- Older cats lose muscle tone, their skin loses elasticity and the coat becomes thinner. They may be reluctant to go outside in the cold, so even if they have always gone outside to toilet in the past, consider using a litter tray, particularly at night, to avoid accidents.

- For the same reason as above, you can keep your cat cosy and warm at night by treating him to a warmer bed next to a radiator and in a draught-free area. If the weather is particularly cold he may appreciate a well-covered hot water bottle to keep the chills away and to stop his joints from stiffening up quite as much.

- Remember that older cats tend to lose their sense of taste and smell, so tempt them to eat by introducing a few strong-smelling prawns or a tasty piece of chicken into their food. Some owners report that making their own meat jelly is a great success. Simply drain off any juice after roasting a chicken or joint of meat and, when it is cool, put it in the refrigerator to set. You can then scrape off the fat from the top and be left with the meat jelly, which many cats find delicious as an occasional treat.

- Invest in a raised stand for your cat's food and water bowls. He will appreciate not having to bend down low in order to eat. Take care that the stand is not positioned too high for him, though, as putting his neck at an awkward angle could be very painful.

- Negotiating the cat flap can become a problem. If you notice that your cat is struggling to get in and out, consider tying the door up for him during the daytime.

- Try to engage your cat in some gentle play sessions to keep him mentally and physically active. If in the past he enjoyed leaping from chair to chair or racing up and down the stairs he may well continue to try doing this but risk injuring himself. Instead, roll a ball for him or drag a screwed up piece of paper in a figure of eight direction to assist mobility. Laying a treasure trail of tiny food treats can encourage him to walk around the room looking for them.

- Resist moving the furniture around too much, particularly if your cat is partially sighted or blind. He will be familiar with the present arrangement and may find any changes very disorienting.

- Look on the bright side! If your cat was always terrified of fireworks, he may not hear them as well in old age and sleep right through the loudest of displays.
- Your older cat will appreciate a bean bag or two to rest his old bones on. They are perfect because of the way they absorb body shape and help to provide warmth and support. Make sure that you do not get one that is too big for him to climb up onto easily. Bean bags are available to buy commercially or, if you are handy with a needle and thread, are very easy to make. Make an extra cover for the bag with a zip or Velcro fastening so that you can take it off and wash it when necessary.
- Keep a close eye on your older cat in hot weather. He may really enjoy sunbathing but if he falls asleep and lies there for too long he may be prone to dehydration or the development of sunburn or even skin cancers. It is sensible to keep the cat in a cooler, shaded area during the hottest part of the day.
- Stretching up to claw at scratching posts or tree trunks can become problematic. Check your cat's claws regularly and trim if necessary (see page 119).
- Research has shown that increased levels of Omega-3 oils can help keep joints pain free, supple and mobile, as well as helping to maintain a healthy heart and circulation. Ask your vet whether he advises feeding supplements to help improve your cat's mobility.
- Be aware that older cats can sometimes become a little disoriented, so supervise your cat more when he is outside in the garden to ensure that he does not wander off and get lost.
- Dry your cat thoroughly if he returns home wet after being outside in the garden.

Making the final decision

Despite all your best efforts and all the love and attention you lavish on your cat throughout his life, you cannot hold back the hands of time for ever. As your cat's life draws to a close, he may simply die in his sleep one day or you may be forced to come to the difficult decision to euthanase the cat and put a stop to any suffering he is enduring. Most owners tend to put these decisions off as long as they possibly can, but sometimes a cat has such a poor quality of life that it can be very upsetting to see them struggle on day after day. A responsible owner will always do what is best for the animal, rather than for themselves.

Your vet has been trained to help owners deal with this difficult and emotive subject but although he can advise you, at the end of the day no one should put pressure on an owner. Sometimes a decision is very straightforward, particularly if the cat has been involved in a road accident or is very badly injured. Other cases are more complicated and factors such as timing, age and quality of life need to be considered. Try to involve everyone in the family in the decision-making process, including children, as this will help them to come to terms with the reality of losing a pet.

When you are talking about the quality of your cat's life, and deciding whether or not he is suffering too much, there are some questions for you to consider:

- Can he eat and drink normally?
- Is he able to breathe properly?
- Can he empty his bowels and bladder normally?
- Is your cat in severe, untreatable pain?
- Is he totally incontinent?
- Has he become so blind and/or deaf that he cannot cope with everyday living?
- Has your cat become such a financial and/or emotional burden that you are no longer able to cope with caring for him properly?

If the answer to any of the final four questions is yes, then you should probably consider the humane option of euthanasia. Euthanasia, sometimes referred to as 'putting to sleep', is a quick and painless procedure that is carried out by vets. Depending on the circumstances you maybe able to have this done at home if this is what you prefer, or it may be done at the surgery where your vet has all the equipment and staff that he needs.

Burial or cremation?

As painful as it may be, take a few minutes before your cat is put to sleep to consider what you would like to happen to his body. You may be too upset to discuss this later on and just wish to leave the surgery as quickly as you possibly can. There are several options available to you. You can leave the cat at the surgery, and the staff will arrange for his body to be frozen until he is collected for cremation. If you prefer, you can take the cat home with you and bury him in your garden, although you need to dig a hole that is at least 60 cm deep and you may need permission from your local authority. An alternative to this is to have your pet buried at a licensed pet cemetery, but you may need to investigate this before euthanasia so that you can telephone them on the day to make arrangements for them to collect the cat. Many people opt to have their cat cremated, but if you want to get his ashes returned to you, make certain that you inform your vet at the time of euthanasia so that he can ensure this is what happens.

Euthanasia

If a cat has always been nervous about going to the surgery your vet may prescribe a sedative to relax him before you leave home so that he is totally calm and unaware of anything stressful throughout. Most appointments for euthanasia will be arranged for the beginning or end of a clinic, so that owners are not expected to wait.

When you arrive at the surgery your vet will ask you to sign a consent form. He will then shave a little piece of fur from one of the cat's front paws and inject him with an overdose of a drug, similar to an anaesthetic. Within seconds your cat will fall into a deep sleep and will not feel any more pain or fear. A few seconds later his heart and lungs will stop and your vet will listen to his chest through a stethescope to ensure that he has passed away.

If you can be present during the procedure your cat will probably appreciate your familiar presence but if you feel unable to cope or are certain you will sob uncontrollably it may be better to allow a veterinary nurse to take over so that the cat does not pick up on your distress. Owners should never feel guilty about not being strong enough to be present during euthanasia, it is a very common reaction and one that is completely understandable. Take comfort in knowing that you did everything possible for your cat throughout each stage of his life and protecting him from seeing your distress was just another part of this. It is commendable to ensure your cat has a good quality of life but equally commendable to do the right thing and ensure he has a good quality of death as well.

Coping with bereavement

It can take owners a long time to get over the loss of a cat, particularly if they have owned him for many years. Some people grieve as much as they would for the loss of a human friend and should not feel embarrassed about doing so. Returning home to an empty house without your beloved cat can be truly heartbreaking. The grieving process will take as long as it takes, whether that is weeks, months or even years but ensure you talk things through with sympathetic friends or people who know what you are going through. Some veterinary nurses have been trained as bereavement counsellors and if you feel unable to cope with your grief do not hesitate to make an appointment to see them and talk through how you are feeling. It is very important to be careful who you talk to, as unsympathetic people who tell you 'it was only a cat' and advise you to 'pull yourself together' will only make things a whole lot worse because it will not allow you to fully express your grief and begin to recover.

Research into grieving shows that there are several stages that everyone has to go through in order to begin to heal. These are:

- **Anticipated loss** – This is experienced with a prolonged illness or euthanasia. Owners start to say goodbye to their cat and may begin to emotionally detach themselves in preparation of their loss.
- **Shock and denial** – This is often experienced immediately after death, although there may be an initial feeling of relief if a cat has been suffering a great deal.
- **Emotional pain and suffering** – These are the middle phases of a grief reaction.
- **Recovery** – This is when owners begin to accept what has happened and find meaning and comfort in thinking about the life and death of their cat.

The Pet Bereavement Support Service (PBSS), run by the Blue Cross animal welfare charity, and the Society for Companion Animal Studies (SCAS) offer telephone and email support to bereaved pet owners. For more information you can visit their website at: www.bluecross.org.uk. There are many similar pet grief support groups in the USA such as www.petsupport.net or your vet may advise on a local bereavement counsellor.

When you are feeling better (which can take many months) you may feel able to help out as a befriender, sharing the wisdom of your experiences with someone else who is grieving for a cat they have lost.

Helping children cope

The loss of a pet cat can often be a child's first experience of death, and it is important to consider their age and level of emotional maturity as you help them cope with the situation. Be gentle but also honest as you explain what has happened. Hopefully, if the cat was euthanased they will have been involved in the decision-making process but if a cat was involved in a road traffic accident and died unexpectedly they will obviously feel as shocked as you do. Thankfully children have a huge capacity to cope with situations and many appear to recover more quickly than adults.

When talking to children try to avoid the phrases 'put to sleep' or 'he went to sleep and never woke up again' as this can make young children afraid to go to sleep in case they do not wake up again either.

It can be helpful for everyone in the family to think of ways to remember the cat. Ask the children to make suggestions and encourage them to talk about how they are feeling.

Suggestions can include:

• Writing a story or poem about the pet.
• Planting a tree or special plant in the cat's favourite part of the garden.
• Making a scrap book or collage of photographs.
• Putting a bench in the garden with an engraved plaque or a memorial close by so that you can sit and remember him in quiet times.

Some families have found it helpful to organize a simple farewell ceremony. This can involve the burial or scattering of ashes or the planting of a shrub, with the children saying a few words about the cat. But however you decide to say goodbye, it is inevitable that your children will want to continue talking about what has happened to the cat and be given the opportunity to do so at any time.

Here is a poem written to comfort bereaved owners that is ideal for children to read at a goodbye ceremony.

Rainbow Bridge

When an animal dies that has been especially close to someone here, that pet goes to Rainbow Bridge. There are meadows and hills for all of our special friends so they can run and play together. There is plenty of food, water and sunshine, and our friends are warm and comfortable.

All the animals who had been ill and old are restored to health and vigour. Those who were hurt or maimed are made whole and strong again, just as we remember them in our dreams of days and times gone by. The animals are happy and content, except for one small thing; they each miss someone very special to them who had to be left behind.

They all run and play together, but the day comes when one suddenly stops and looks into the distance. His bright eyes are intent his eager body quivers. Suddenly he begins to run from the group, flying over the green grass, his legs carrying him faster and faster.

You have been spotted, and when you and your special friend finally meet, you cling together in joyous reunion, never to be parted again. The happy kisses rain upon your face; your hands again caress the beloved head, and you look once more into the trusting eyes of your pet, so long gone from your life but never absent from your heart.

Then you cross Rainbow Bridge together.

(Author unknown)

Cats and grief

There is some evidence that in a multi-cat household some cats appear to experience grief at the loss of a companion – even if they did not particularly get on well with them when they were alive. Every cat is different and some will show no signs of grief, while others will appear depressed, lose their appetite and change their sleep patterns, etc. It is not known whether they are reacting to their owner's distress, the loss of a friend, or a combination of both. Either way, it is important not to react too much to these kinds of behavioural changes as to do so will reinforce and prolong the situation. Try not to constantly pick the cat up and comfort him, it is much better to keep to your regular routine as much as possible and in time things will return to normal.

It has to be said that if the cat that died was the dominant cat in the house the remaining puss may blossom and flourish in his new role of top cat. You may find that he 'comes out of his shell' and enjoys all the fuss and attention he is now receiving!

When to get another cat

Sooner or later your initial grief will ease and you may start thinking that your life is much too empty without a cat to love and care for. Some people decide to get another cat almost immediately, particularly if they have had an older pet and more time to prepare themselves for the inevitable. Other people think they can never love another cat as much as the first one and cannot face the heartbreak of losing one again. However, it is not an act of disloyalty to think about getting another cat, and could be very therapeutic to do so. In time you will be able to bond with and love another cat in a completely different way. It is important to take as much time as you need before replacing a cat that has died, and not cave in to pressure from other family members, but once you are able to smile at happy memories of the times you and your cat shared together, then you may well be able to open your heart and your home to another beautiful feline friend.

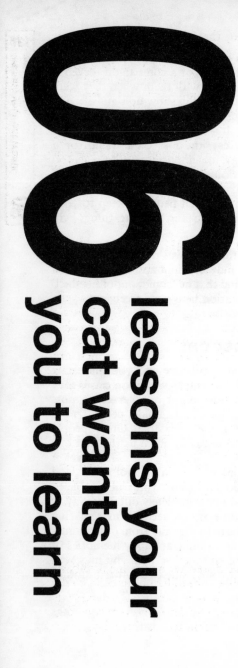

06
lessons your cat wants you to learn

In this chapter you will learn:
- how to prevent diseases
- how to better understand your cat
- how to be the perfect owner.

As you have probably realized, there is a great deal to learn about living with and looking after a cat. Of course you can just provide him with the basics – a roof over his head, food to eat and water to drink – and he may survive but to give him a rich, fulfilled and happy life there are many lessons to learn. The more you put into the relationship you have with your cat, the more you will get out of it. You can experience the fun of playing with him, the communication between you, the companionship, the trust and the amazing bond that can develop. Cats are such free spirits (some might say fickle!) that when they choose to befriend you, rather than simply tolerate you, it makes the relationship even more special.

Lesson 1 When to vaccinate?

It is not clear what the exact duration of immunity to disease offered by vaccinations is and therefore booster injections are usually advised. Vets normally recommend vaccinating cats with three or four 'core' vaccines and then making a lifestyle judgement to determine whether or not a cat requires other 'non-core' vaccines to provide protection from diseases that he may not be at significant risk from. Core vaccines are herpesvirus, calcivirus and feline panleukopenia. Outdoor cats are also at risk of developing feline leukaemia and so this is also considered to be a core vaccine for them.

Some owners are worried about cats suffering from adverse reactions to vaccines but research shows that incidences of this are extremely low. Most vets consider that the benefits of giving booster vaccines to protect pets against potentially fatal diseases far outweigh any risks involved. Cats that will go into a boarding kennel or into a show ring must keep their booster injections up to date.

Feline panleukopenia

This is also referred to as feline distemper and feline infectious enteritis and used to be the number one killer of cats prior to the development of a safe vaccine. It is a particularly dangerous disease for kittens and young cats, who develop severe vomiting, diarrhoea and fatal dehydration within two to three days.

Cat flu

This is also referred to as feline viral rhinotracheitis and is caused by feline calcivirus and herpesvirus. It is rarely fatal except in very young or very old cats, or those that are suffering from another disease. Symptoms are similar to those experienced by humans, i.e. runny nose and eyes, sneezing, etc., but there may be also be the development of painful mouth ulcers. Once a cat has been exposed to the virus he will become a carrier and can infect other unvaccinated cats.

Feline leukaemia virus (FeLV)

Unfortunately, once a cat is infected with FeLV he remains so for life and will usually go on to develop the fatal disease. Infection with FeLV has been controlled in recent years by continued testing for the virus and isolating infected cats from non-infected cats.

Rabies

If you are intending to travel abroad with your cat he will need rabies injections in order to comply with the Pet Travel Scheme. The rabies virus can, among other things, attack the nervous system and cause potentially fatal disease.

Lesson 2 When to worm?

All pets are likely to be affected by worms at some stage in their life and many will become re-infected unless they are given regular routine worming treatments. Thankfully, it is relatively easy and inexpensive to get rid of worms and regular treatments are therefore recommended. Kittens should be treated for worms every two weeks from the age of six weeks to 16 weeks and older outdoor cats may need to be treated every three to six months depending on their lifestyle. If cats are prolific hunters they may need to be treated more often. Indoor cats may never be exposed to worms and may not need repeated treatments after the worms have been eliminated as a kitten. It is advisable to discuss treatment of worms with your vet to check that you are protecting your cat as much as he needs.

If you are intending to travel abroad with your cat he will require treatment for tapeworms 24–48 hours prior to travelling back to the UK in order to prevent disease from being imported back into the country.

> **Top Cat Tip**
>
> If your cat uses your garden as a toilet, clean up any faeces that you find, sealing it in a plastic bag and disposing of it in your dustbin. This will help to reduce the risk of worm eggs hatching. Always encourage children to wash their hands thoroughly after playing in the garden.

Lesson 3 When to treat for fleas?

According to vets, flea infestation is the number one cause of skin disease that they treat in cats. Allergy to fleas and skin irritation are very common and the best way to avoid this is to treat the cat for fleas all year round. Centrally heated homes and multi-cat households are sheer heaven to fleas!

How often you treat your cat and your home for fleas will depend on the product you use. Some products require treatment once every three months, some oral products are administered monthly and some treatments are administered on a weekly basis. The key to successful treatment is to follow the manufacturer's guidelines as closely as possible. Your vet will advise on the most suitable treatment for your cat.

> **Top Cat Tip**
>
> Remember that alternative flea treatments do not kill fleas but will only help to repel them.

Lesson 4 Be observant!

There is no one that is better qualified to notice or suspect that something is wrong with your cat than you, the owner. Get into the habit of watching him so that you know how he walks normally, how he usually feeds, what his sleeping patterns are and how he behaves when he is handled. Having a gut instinct that something is wrong is a good enough reason to seek veterinary advice as very often vets find that the owner is absolutely correct and tests prove there is indeed a problem that your cat will appreciate some help with.

Lesson 5 Be aware

Get into the habit of knowing where your cat is! Statistics show that in the UK, around 15,000 people a year require hospital treatment because of an accident at home involving their cat. Most cases involve scratches and bites that need medical attention, while others involve injuries sustained when people have tripped over their cat. First-time cat owners in particular need to get used to having a cat around, and be aware that they do tend to slink around your feet, particularly if they are waiting to be fed or want you to open the door for them to go outside. You can try to clicker train your cat to sit and wait for his food or for you to open the door, but be aware that cats move quickly and quietly and can sneak up on you unawares, which is when you are vulnerable to a fall.

Lesson 6 What cats hate about going into the cattery

Actually, if you take the time and trouble to find a really good cattery and your cat has been well socialized he should at least tolerate, if not enjoy, his stay. The problem is that cats are creatures of habit and they really do not like having their routines disrupted and can find this quite stressful. Being physically removed from everything they know to a strange place where all their familiar territorial markings are missing can be traumatic, particularly if a cat is a timid, sensitive personality type. Some cats seem oblivious and provided they are fed on time, have a warm bed to sleep in and a sunny spot for a snooze they sail through the whole experience. If you have two cats ask if they can be boarded together, so that they can reassure each other by grooming and sleeping next to each other. Take their own toys and blankets in so that these can comfort them too.

Lesson 7 What cats hate about coming home again!

Some cats can react quite strangely when they return home from the cattery. Quite often owners are heard to say, 'He was really angry with me and sulked for a week!' Of course cats are not equipped with the same emotions as humans and will not be reacting towards their owners with anger.

Cats live very much in the moment and are not thinking about how much they disliked their time in the cattery and how they can exact their revenge. They will simply be trying to adjust to coming home again, and finding that those once-familiar smells have faded or changed since they have been away. Their sense of wellbeing will be temporarily disrupted and until this has been re-established you may find they are slightly self-obsessed and aloof or may go to the other extreme and become very clingy and over-dependent on their owners. Some cats will make a huge effort to re-establish their scent by indulging in indoor spraying, scratching or face rubbing on and around the furniture. Try not to reinforce strange behaviour patterns by paying a lot of attention to them. Rewarding aloof or clingy behaviour with lots of cuddles, treats or other attention will only prolong the situation. Get back into your usual routine as quickly as possible things will return to normal much more quickly.

Some cats will benefit from the use of a plug-in pheromone spray in the home, to help reduce their stress levels (see Chapter 04, page 93 for more information on these).

Top Cat Tip

If your cat suffers a severe reaction to returning home from the cattery it may be less stressful to find alternative arrangements for him the next time you have to go away. Consider employing a pet-sitter or asking a neighbour or family friend to call in and look after the cat two or three times a day.

Lesson 8 Don't worry, be happy ...

One very important lesson your cat will want you to learn is the importance of maintaining a stress-free environment. Remember, what you consider to be stress-free may not necessarily be acceptable to your cat, particularly if he lives in a multi-cat household where shared space and living conditions can be very stressful. Burning candles, relaxing in the bath and playing Mozart may work for you but a cat needs to be able to find his inner calm in other ways. Ensure he has access to high areas such as on top of a cupboard or an activity centre where he can safely observe what is going on in the house. He will also need safety zones that he can get to whenever he feels threatened, such as behind the sofa or under a chair. Do not deprive him of any of these places by dragging him out to join the rest of the family, but instead leave him to calm down and come out in his own time. It is also very important in a multi-cat household to have plenty of litter trays, so that no cat is bullied away from one at any time. Ensure that litter trays are kept clean and make sure that there are lots of feeding stations and water bowls.

Provide your cat with lots of attention, entertainment and physical stimulation to prevent boredom setting in. See Chapter 03 for suggestions of games you can play.

Lesson 9 Stamp out bullying

No one likes a bully and they can be very difficult to live with. If you keep more than one cat it is natural for one to be more dominant than the other but distressing if a cat is being intimidated so much that his life becomes a misery. In worst-case scenarios some bullied cats choose to live outside, refusing to come inside except to be fed, and, given the opportunity, will go off to find themselves alternative accommodation with a friendly neighbour!

Unlike humans, cats do not thrive in a mutually co-operative society and prefer to rely on themselves for survival. This does not mean that cats are incapable of forming a close relationship with another cat, but many factors will influence their ability to do so, including early experiences during the first few weeks of their lives as kittens.

Behaviourists report that one of the most common reasons they are consulted is when one cat in a household is terrorizing another. Assessing the available resources and providing all the cats in the house with sufficient litter trays, food and water bowls, beds, toys, observation platforms, scratching posts and areas they can hide in are key factors to preventing bullying.

If a neighbouring cat is bullying your cat when he is out in his own garden, ensure that he has access to a cat flap that only he can get through so that if he feels threatened he is able to escape confrontation and injury.

> **Top Cat Tip**
>
> You can help deter a bullying neighbourhood cat from coming into your garden by aiming a single squirt from a water pistol. This will help to reinforce that your garden is not a nice place for him to be. If possible, do this from an upstairs window so that the cat associates this unpleasant experience with coming into your garden rather than with the humans who live there.

> **Top Cat Tip**
>
> If you are forced to confront the fact that your cat *is* the neighbourhood bully (oh, the shame!) then have a chat with your neighbours to find out what time their cats go out so that you can keep yours indoors at these times. Putting a collar with a bell on will also help alert other cats that he is on the prowl before they actually see him, giving them a chance to escape.

Lesson 10 What makes a finicky feline

We have dealt with obesity and the dangers of allowing your cat to become overweight but it can be very tiresome and stressful if you are unable to tempt your cat into eating the food you provide. If this behaviour develops suddenly there may be a medical problem that will explain it so take him to the vet for a thorough check-up. Ask your vet to weigh the cat and then take him back in a month's time to see if he is losing any weight. Once he has the all clear you can begin to address the problem. Fussy eaters are usually the product of over-attentive owners who have pandered to all their demands by offering endless supplies of ever-more-tempting meals and treats. One behaviourist was asked to see an owner who provided seven varieties of food for her cat at every mealtime, just in case the cat disliked a particular flavour on that day. Another lady was completely worn out from getting up at 3 a.m. to cook fish for her cat because she thought that he was asking her for it! Do not fall into the trap of smothering your cat with too much love, as it will ultimately hurt you and your cat. The best advice is to choose a good quality complete balanced food and stick to it.

Be a copy cat!

Finally, there are several valuable lessons that we owners can begin to learn from our cats. Why not take a leaf from his book and try out a few feline strategies to help bring your stress levels down and make your life more enjoyable? Of course, just like our cats, we are all different – some of us are placid Persian types and others are more vocal and need a lot of entertaining, like the higher maintenance Siamese! Here are some behaviour traits that all our cats have in common and that we owners could do well to adopt:

The art of relaxation

Cats can spend 16 hours a day sleeping, and while this might be a little excessive for us humans, we could all benefit from a power nap or two during the day. Unlike us, cats instinctively know what is good for them and they will not sit in their basket worrying about where their next meal is coming from or why they are not sleeping. Stressed-out owners are often suffering from serious sleep deprivation and if you are not sleeping properly, do something about it!

Fine dining

Healthy cats eat regular meals and enjoy a balanced, complete diet, which is washed down with fresh water. They then usually settle down for a little siesta or a quiet few minutes until the food has been digested. We, on the other hand, tend to grab a sandwich or an unhealthy fast food snack, eat it on the run, go straight back to work and then wonder why we are suffering from indigestion and gastric upsets.

Pampering

Cats are real experts when it comes to looking after themselves. They will spend inordinate amounts of time ensuring that they look their very best at all times. Just sitting down with your cat and stroking him can help bring down your blood pressure but the emotional lift you will get from taking time to book yourself a massage, a manicure or a new hair cut can also do wonders for your self-esteem.

Communication

We may not always understand how our cats communicate but one thing is certain, they are always trying their best to let us know how they feel. Each type of behaviour they display can give you an insight into their state of mind. For example, if your cat has had enough of being groomed or stroked he will soon tell you, either vocally or by removing himself from the situation. In some cases, if he is feeling impatient he might even use his claws or teeth to demonstrate his displeasure! If a stressful situation arises such as a visit to the vet, he will not hesitate to communicate his disapproval. Cats instinctively know the importance of letting people know how they are feeling, so that something can be done about the situation. We owners could learn a lot from their refusal to tolerate something they find stressful.

It is unrealistic to think that we can eliminate all stress from the lives of our cats or ourselves. After all, some stress is known to be good for us; it helps us to recognize and react to real or perceived dangers. However, prolonged stress from continued exposure to these dangerous situations is unhealthy for everyone. Stressed cats will react by exhibiting behaviour patterns that we consider to be problematic but to them are perfectly logical. It is only by trying to learn as much as we can about ourselves and our cats that we can begin to understand and respect each other better. Hopefully, we can then all learn to live together in 'purrfect' harmony!

taking it further

Useful contacts

Association of Pet Behaviour Counsellors: www.apbc.org.uk

Bengal Cat Club of Great Britain: www.bengalcat.org.uk

Birman Cat Club: www.birmancatclub.co.uk

Blue Cross: www.bluecross.org.uk

British Ragdoll Cat Club: www.tbrcc.co.uk

British Shorthair Cat Club: www.britishshorthaircatclub.co.uk

Burmese Cat Club: www.burmesecatclub.com

Cat Fanciers Association: www.cfainc.org

Cats Protection: www.cats.org.uk

Chinchilla, Silver Tabby and Smoke Cat Society:
www.cat-society-chinchilla.org.uk

Clicker training: www.clickertraining.co.uk

Colourpoint Persian Cat Club: www.colourpointcatclub.co.uk

Exotic Shorthair Cat Society:
www.exoticshorthaircatsociety.co.uk

Feline Advisory Bureau: www.fabcats.org

Felis Britannica: www.felisbritannica.co.uk

Governing Council of the Cat Fancy: www.gccfcats.org

Maine Coon Cat Club: www.maine-coon-cat-club.com

Oriental Cat Association: www.oca-cats.org.uk

PDSA: www.pdsa.org.uk

Rex Cat Club: www.rexcatassociation.org.uk

Royal Society for the Prevention of Cruelty to Animals: www.rspca.org.uk

Sacred Cat of Burma Fanciers: www.scbf.com

Sphynx Cat Club: www.sphynxcatclub.co.uk

The International Bengal Cat Society: www.bengalcat.com

TTEAM: www.tilleyfarm.co.uk or www.tteam-ttouch.com

United States Department of Agriculture: www.aphis.usda.gov

index

teach
yourself

dog training
association of pet dog trainers

- Do you want a comprehensive guide to training your dog?
- Would you like your dog to be socially well-behaved?
- Do you need advice on all aspects of being a dog owner?

If you want your dog to be well-behaved then **Dog Training** is for you. Essential reading for all dog owners or those thinking of buying a dog for the first time, this book covers every aspect of kind, fair and effective dog training as well as authoritative advice on looking after your pet. Using positive, reward and motivational techniques, including clicker training, you will be able to train your dog to be obedient, sociable and, most importantly, to be a part of your family.

Association of Pet Dog Trainers offers pet dog owners a guarantee of quality when looking for dog training advice. The APDT abide by kind and fair principles of training and have written this book accordingly. For more information, visit www.apdt.co.uk

teach yourself

keeping poultry
victoria roberts

- Do you want to know which breed lays best?
- Would you like advice on housing and equipment?
- Are you considering keeping ducks and geese?

Whether you want to start from scratch with a few hens, or branch into ducks, geese and other birds, **Keeping Poultry** is for you. It tells you which breed of bird lays best and gives useful guidance on housing, equipment and the necessities of day-to-day care. Covering all types of poultry, this guide offers advice on everything from exhibiting birds to meat production, with a full 'trouble-shooting' section and even tips for breeding your birds.

Victoria Roberts, BVSc MRCVS, is the author or editor of five books on keeping poultry, the Honorary Veterinary Surgeon for the Poultry Club, and the Editor of the Poultry Club newsletter.

teach yourself

owning a horse
carolyn henderson

- Do you want to know how to buy a horse?
- Would you like practical advice on grooming?
- Would you like to find out about horse psychology?

Owning a Horse is aimed at all those interested in buying and keeping their own horse, whether at home or in a yard. It covers not only day-to-day care from tack to feeding, but also explains costs, which breed to choose, and all the formalities of buying and insuring. Authoritative yet readable, with plenty of helpful resources, it is an essential guide for would-be owners.

Carolyn Henderson is a journalist and author. She has written over 20 books on all aspects of horse care, her articles appear regularly in *Horse and Hound*, *Horse and Rider* and *Horse*, and she has wide experience of keeping, schooling and competing horses.